Exploring The Mason Dixon Line

Exploring The Mason Dixon Line

Walking In The Footsteps Of History

Jack Layton

American History Imprints / American History Press
Franklin, Tennessee
www.Americanhistoryimprints.com
www.Americanhistorypress.com
Book design by Chris Keegan
Index by Francis E. Ferguson

ISBN 10: 0-9842256-4-1
ISBN 13: 978-0-9842256-4-4

First Edition April 2010

Library of Congress Control Number: 209937915

Printed in the United States of America on acid-free paper
This book meets all ANSI standards for archival quality.

Table Of Contents

WESTWARD HO

THE NORTH LINE

PUSHING THE LINE WEST

1766 - NORTH MOUNTAIN AND BEYOND

⊷ Foreword ⊷

Jack Layton's book tracing the historic survey of Charles Mason and Jeremiah Dixon from the time they arrived in the Americas in 1763 until they planted their last marker in 1767 is a welcome addition to every American's library. With vivid imagery, detailed descriptions, and photographs he documents the story of the two Englishmen who changed American history forever. This book will spur you into putting your hiking boots on and heading out the door, to see for yourself the many sites along the line that might appeal to your curiosity. Discovering the ancient boundary markers in deep woods is a lasting memory that you will treasure, and reading the historical markers along the route will give you a real sense of how each generation interprets its heritage.

Among many other pertinent details, Layton has explained in straightforward language the complexities involved in trying to draw straight lines on the Earth's irregular curving surface. The mathematics and geometry are not for the fainthearted, but those who try will enjoy the satisfaction of resolving the angles of the horizon plane and surface irregularities, as well as those of the earth's orbit and celestial sphere. This book will also encourage you to study your own property line surveys and the historic events that may be associated with them.

History is a fascinating but shadowy subject. Especially poignant is the association of the Mason Dixon Line with the great tragedy of the War Between the States. Even though the survey took place almost 100 years before the Civil War, many Americans immediately identify the Mason Dixon Line as the de facto boundary between the territories of the slave and free states. However, the lands of present-day West Virginia, a state that did not subscribe to slavery, are totally south of the survey line. With but minor exception, Layton avoids intertwining the war with the line as he goes about telling the story of the two British surveyors and mathematicians as they measured and marked their way across the 18th century wilderness of Maryland and Pennsylvania.

After you've read this book, schedule some time to visit the sections of the line that interest you. Make an effort to uncover the local history and sites along your route, and you'll soon discover how the present is shaped by the past. It is a continual battle to preserve historic places and leave a balanced record of history, and Jack Layton's record of his unique trek along the line will certainly assist in that effort.

Richard Little, Ph.D.
Associate Professor of Geography (Ret.)
West Virginia University

⇥ INTRODUCTION ⇤

My wife, Cathy, has affectionately dubbed it "The Good Old Boys' Club." That is her way of describing a group of men who have been meeting, for who knows how long, at a local eating emporium called the *Eat 'N Park*. The club lacks a charter, and has no by-laws, dues, or club officers. There is, however, a special spot in the restaurant known as the "Table of Knowledge," where the club holds court almost every weekday morning. Membership is by invitation only, but once asked to sit at the table, you are forever welcome.

The unacknowledged purpose of the club is for male bonding. Women, however, are not entirely excluded, and from time to time one of the members' wives will join us in our lively discussions. Mary, Celeste and Rose—long-time waitresses at *Eat 'N Park*—know the group well. They sometimes—either by invitation or otherwise—proffer their opinion about the topic of the day, which may vary from politics to medicine to science to sports to personal views on any subject that strikes one's fancy.

Regular members during the fifteen years since I was first invited to sit at the esteemed table have included Henry, a printer who passed away a few years ago; Jim, a retired apple farmer who is now in his 80s; Sherm, a surgeon; Guy, a dentist; Ed, the local two-way radio man; Larry, a surveyor; Pat, a metal tubing salesman; yours truly, Jack-of-all-trades, master-of-none; and last, but by no means least, Sam, the hearing-aid man.

Sam Lybarger passed away in early 2001 at about ninety-years-old. He held many patents for various hearing-aid devices, owned a business where he manufactured them, and formerly taught electronics at Carnegie Mellon University. Sam was a ham radio operator way back in the 1920s, when it was considered to be the "hobby of wizards." It is Sam to whom I dedicate this book, for without him it would not have been written.

Sam was a true gentleman who could find the solution to almost any scientific question and then explain it to you in understandable terms. He could shed light on the most puzzling of problems by producing documentation to prove or disprove discussions that crossed the threshold of the morning breakfast table.

Does average sea level vary at different points on the surface of our planet? It certainly does, and the morning after it was the topic of discussion, Sam appeared with a half-dozen pages copied from a book written by a Russian author that shed light on all of the pieces of the puzzle. Were there ever cable cars in the streets of Pittsburgh? Sure enough, there were. Sam showed up the next day with Xerox® copies of pages that showed their routes of travel, the power of the motors that drove the underground cables, and the dates of their construction and ultimate demise.

The subject that sparked my interest in the Mason Dixon Line came up at the table one morning: Why does the southern border of Pennsylvania end on its west end in a wooded ravine in the middle of nowhere, and then turn abruptly north? Logically, it would seem to make more sense if the southern boundary line of the state continued a few miles further west to the Ohio River. Sam had the answer. The next day he produced copies of records that detailed the limits of William Penn's 1681 land grant from King Charles II of England. The answer to the question of the day: The bounds of Penn's province, as granted by the original charter, extended westward for five degrees in longitude from the banks of the Delaware River, and no further.

I have always been fascinated by the boundaries that define the borders of the various states. I was born in southern New Jersey, just across the Delaware River from Philadelphia, and I grew up in the area. This mighty body of water, almost a mile across at that point, marks the dividing line between Pennsylvania and New Jersey. It is a tangible geographic mark on the surface of the earth that is easy to observe, so it makes sense that it should form the boundary between two states. But one day, when I was a young boy, we took a vacation across the mighty waterway west to Pennsylvania, and then south across an invisible line into the state of Delaware, and finally across another invisible line into the state of Maryland. Why were these invisible dividing lines in these particular spots and not in another? As a preteen, this puzzled and fascinated me. It seemed almost magical that I could stand beside a stone boundary line marker and have one foot in Delaware and the other in Maryland!

Sam's few copied pages rekindled my old fascination with these invisible dividing lines on the surface of the earth. In particular, I became intrigued with the southern border of Pennsylvania. Why was it laid out in that particular place? How did it originally come about? How accurate is the placement of the visible indicators along this invisible line? What would it be like to travel the entire distance of this line first made visible by stone markers placed by the now-famous Charles Mason and Jeremiah Dixon?

That was back in 1990. I filed the information that Sam provided in a 3-inch-thick loose-leaf binder. From time to time, as I would come across additional information about the Mason Dixon Line, I would add it to what was already in the binder. Occasionally, when I heard something on the subject that seemed interesting, I would scribble some handwritten notes, and into the binder they would go. Before long, there was no more room. A second 3-inch binder was added, followed by a third and fourth and fifth. Today there are eight 3-inch binders marked **MASON DIXON**, chock full of information, sitting on my bookshelf. Eventually, I decided that I would like to share this information with other people who might have some of the same interest and fascination with this invisible line—the line that separates the Commonwealth of Pennsylvania from the states of Maryland and West Virginia—the great dividing line of latitude called the Mason Dixon Line.

As I continued my research about the boundary, originally blazed by two English surveyors and astronomers, I discovered that the lands that today make up the state of Delaware were also once part of the Penn family's province. They were called the Lower Three Counties, and the 82-mile-long, north-south dividing line that separated them from those claimed by the Calvert family of Maryland was also surveyed and marked by Mason and Dixon.

As I gathered my information in bits and pieces, I attempted to convey some of my enthusiasm to friends and colleagues. Immediately upon hearing the words "Mason Dixon Line", the almost universal reply would be, "Sure, that's the line that divided North from South—slave from free states—during the Civil War." However, the drawing and marking of the line had nothing to do with slave and free states. As a matter of fact, it was surveyed and marked a decade before the United States of America even existed, and the line was almost 100 years old when the Civil War erupted. The east-west portion of the line as surveyed by Mason and Dixon is only 233 miles long, and its western limit does not even extend to the western border of Pennsylvania. In the course of my research, I came across many historical markers, books, Internet papers and articles that would lead one to believe that this dividing line originates in New Jersey and has its western terminus somewhere in Kansas! In addition, every square foot of the territory that makes up the state of West Virginia is south of the survey line. This land, carved out of what was formerly Virginia, was molded into a state as a consequence of the Civil War—the northwestern counties of Virginia did not accept slavery, and split off to form their own state.

In the summer of 2001, I decided to put my thoughts into action by embarking upon the business of traveling the line by visiting as many accessible places along it that I could find. In the process, I would make every effort to correlate the present-day 21st century with the history of the 18th, 19th and 20th centuries, using *The Journal of Charles Mason* as my tour guide. I did not start in the east and work my way west as the British surveyors did. Because I live in southwestern Pennsylvania, the closest point to me on the line is its western terminus. On my first day in the field, I visited the 1883 monument on Browns

Hill, close to where Interstate 79 crosses from Pennsylvania into West Virginia. This monument marks the place where the survey ended, when the Indians accompanying the party declared that this marked the end of their commission to aid the survey crew. From that point on I worked my way eastward, skipping some locales, to come back and explore them at a later date. If a business trip took me to the Philadelphia area, I would try to spend an extra day in the vicinity conducting some on-site exploration. Thus, significant places, such as the *Post Mark'd West* and the *Stargazer Stone*, were visited early on in my efforts, and several were visited on multiple occasions.

Finally, in the spring of 2004, I decided that I would make a final push forward with my project. I resolved in mid-spring to complete my research and my writing by the end of the summer. I took a couple of brief sabbaticals, and all revenue-producing projects were put on hold. I began to redeem many of the thousands of frequent-flyer miles and Holiday Inn Priority Club award points I had accumulated in my many years of business travel as a means of defraying my exploration expenses. Armed with a rough outline of what I wanted to look for and where I wanted to go, I set out on my 21st century adventure of retracing the 18th century enterprise of two English surveyors and their company of men as they traipsed through the wilderness of a vast, untamed North America.

The devices used by the historic survey party included a zenith sector (used to observe the stars to determine latitude), transit instrument (used to measure horizontal angles), Gunter's Chain (used to measure distance), along with horses and horse-drawn wagons for transportation and tents for shelter. Mason brought along a notebook and a writing instrument. On a daily basis, and in meticulous detail, he recorded every facet of their exploits. Excerpts from his journal appear *in italics* throughout this account. For the most part, I have not attempted to make spelling or grammatical corrections to the 18th century English used in documents or his journal entries, except when clarification was necessary.

My modern-day tools would have been totally foreign to the mathematician/astronomer and the surveyor/astronomer who cut their way through the forests, trudged up and down the mountains and slogged across the swamps and waterways of Pennsylvania, Maryland and, what was then, the Province of Virginia. To make a permanent record of my adventures, I used a method called "photography," which of course hadn't been invented in their time. Their determination of position required at least ten clear nights of stellar observations made through the zenith sector—a 6-foot-long, tripod-mounted tube—while lying on the ground. This was followed by a few more days of laborious mathematical calculations to average out any errors. The "stars" I used to determine my position were twenty-four in number, man-made and electronic in nature. They were visible through the heaviest of overcasts, and even at high noon on a sunny day. These mini-electronic wonders, known as NAVSTAR satellites, provided almost instantaneous information to a global positioning receiver, which I carried in a pouch on my belt. It displayed coordinates accurate to within 20-30 feet of where I was standing. This 21st century marvel of technology usually took less than a minute to lock onto the electronic "stars" and calculate my position.

I also employed a full compliment of USGS 7.5 minute typographic maps that detailed every road, trail, stream and mountain that I expected to encounter along every foot of the line with an accuracy far beyond the wildest dreams of a mid-1700s surveyor. As I walked in their footsteps, I marveled at the accuracy of their notations as they documented all of the streams, creeks and mountains that they crossed. All of those measurements appear on today's maps, remarkably close to the distances documented in Mason's journal, and many of the 18th century pathways that the group crossed now have their counterparts in the concrete and asphalt ribbons that comprise modern roads and highways.

My means of transportation was not an animal fueled by hay, but a machine powered by hundreds of virtual horses fueled by distillates from a black-gooey substance that would, almost a century later, be extracted from the ground below some of the land they surveyed. A notebook, writing instrument and a sense of adventure seemed to be the only things that I had in common with these men of two centuries past. However, as I traversed back and forth across the invisible line of longitude known as the Tangent Line, and the great invisible dividing line of latitude now known as the Mason Dixon Line, I felt certain that I was walking right in the tracks of the famous surveyors. I also gained a sense that I knew Charles Mason and Jeremiah Dixon personally, even though the Creator had afforded them their allotted time on this earth more than two centuries removed from mine. The results of my efforts and the judicious use of my inanimate companions—my tools—have resulted in this presentation of my adventures of *walking in the footprints of history*.

Come join me. I invite you to see through my eyes the places they explored and experience some of the history that has taken place along the lines they surveyed in an age long past. Together, let's retrace the footsteps left by Mason and Dixon as they surveyed and made visible two of the invisible dividing lines that separate the colonies of the New World.

Enjoy.
Jack Layton

⸙ PREFACE ⸙

LATITUDE AND LONGITUDE: GEOGRAPHIC COORDINATES

The story about to be told revolves around locating and marking invisible lines on the surface of the earth by strict observation of the path of the stars through the heavens. To enhance one's appreciation of the adventure about to be set forth in words, it is helpful for the reader to have at least a rudimentary understanding of the methods used to describe the locations of these lines and the tools used to establish these locations. From time to time we will take some time out of our travelogue in an attempt to explain in layman's terms the complex science and mathematics used by Mason and Dixon in carrying out their commission.

The third planet distant from the sun—the planet that we call Earth—is roughly the shape of a ball, but in fact it has a slight bulge at the equator. This distortion is due to the forces exerted on it from four billion years of spinning on its axis. For our purposes, though, which is a brief and simple lesson about latitude and longitude, we will consider it to be in the shape of a perfectly round ball. The circumference at the equator of our home planet is approximately 24,900 miles. If we started on a journey at any point on the equator and traveled along it until we were back to the starting point, the distance traveled would be approximately 24,900 miles. Likewise, using the same dimensions, if we started on a journey from the North Pole and traveled directly south, crossing the South Pole, and back up the other side of the earth to our starting point at the North Pole we also would have traveled approximately 24,900 miles.

If we draw ninety equally-spaced horizontal parallel lines from the equator to the North Pole; we can call the equator line zero and number each lines one through ninety. The ninetieth line would actually be just a point—the North Pole itself. In a similar fashion, we can draw another ninety lines from the equator to the South Pole and number them one through ninety. These are called lines of latitude or *parallels* of latitude, for indeed they are parallel and equidistant from one another. They can be further described as being north latitude or south latitude lines, depending on their direction from the equator. In a theoretical journey around the globe, starting at the North Pole, we would cross 360 of these lines—180 on each side of the sphere (90 north of the equator and 90 south of the equator). Each line is one degree in distance from the next by angular measure. By simple arithmetic (24,900 divided by 360) it can easily be determined that

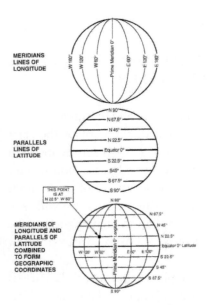

MERIDIANS LINES OF LONGITUDE

PARALLELS LINES OF LATITUDE

MERIDIANS OF LONGITUDE AND PARALLELS OF LATITUDE COMBINED TO FORM GEOGRAPHIC COORDINATES

The grid formed by meridians of longitude combined with parallels of latitude may be used to identify any specific point on the surface of the earth.

there are approximately 69 miles between each of the lines, or that approximately 69 miles in one degree of latitude.

These distances can be refined even further: There are 60 minutes in each degree so there must be (69 divided by 60) approximately 1.15 miles (6072 feet) between each minute of latitude. There are 60 seconds in each minute of latitude so there must be approximately (1.15 divided by 60) .0192 miles (101 feet) in each second of latitude.

One's location north or south of the equator can be determined by observing the relative position of the stars in the sky. Mason and Dixon used this procedure of stellar observation to locate and mark their initial line of latitude, exactly fifteen miles south of the most southern point in the city of Philadelphia.

If we place 360 equally-spaced dots on the equator, using the logic as outlined above, we know that there will be approximately 69 miles between each dot. Now draw a line from the North Pole through each dot on the equator and continue the line to the South Pole. This will result in 360 lines that converge at each pole, each of which is approximately 69 miles apart at the equator. It is important to note that the lines are 69 miles apart only at the equator. Their spacing merges as they travel north or south from the equator, eventually converging at a dot at each pole. These north-south lines are called lines of longitude or *meridians*. Historically, the meridian that runs through Greenwich, England is called the Prime Meridian and is designated as number zero. Successive lines to the east, up to line number 180, are called meridians of east longitude. Those to the west, to line number 180, are meridians of west longitude. The same refinements for distance in minutes and seconds of longitude at the equator can be made as were made for latitude. Again, it is important to keep in mind that the distance of 69 miles between lines of longitude is valid only at the equator. If we wish to determine the distance between meridians at any other place on our sphere a correction factor must be applied. This correction can be factored in using a bit of simple mathematics: The distance between lines of longitude at the equator are multiplied by the cosine of the parallel of latitude north or south of the equator.

Don't let the mathematical parlance scare you. In reality it's quite simple: The line of latitude on which the Mason Dixon Line lays is 39 degrees 43 minutes 19 seconds or approximately 39.75 degrees. The cosine of 39.75 (derived from an electronic slide rule calculator) is 0.77. Therefore the distance between meridians on the Mason Dixon Line is approximately 53 miles (69 x 0.77). The distances between minutes and seconds of longitude on the line are 4675 feet (0.89 miles) and 78 feet respectively.

Determining one's longitude—location east or west of the Prime Meridian—can also be accomplished by observing the stars and the occurrence of celestial events. This, however, requires knowledge of the exact time at the Prime Meridian when the event occurs. Accurate timepieces in the 18th century were not common items, but rather precise scientific instruments.

Note that these lines of latitude (parallels) and longitude (meridians) form an invisible grid on the surface of the Earth. Any point on its surface can be pinpointed by describing its location on the grid—its precise description in degrees, minutes and seconds, either north or south of the equator, and degrees, minutes and seconds either east or west of the Prime Meridian. The location of any point on a sphere, described in this manner, is known as its *geographic coordinate*.

Any location on the globe may be described by referring to its geographic coordinates, as can any point on a typographic map. Parallels of latitude are noted on the vertical edges of such maps, while meridians of longitude are noted on the horizontal edges of the maps. The Global Positioning System (GPS) uses twenty-four NAVSTAR satellites to enable a hand held receiver/computer to read out its position on the earth using this grid of latitude and longitude. GPS accuracy, even with a moderately priced receiver, is to within 10 meters—30 feet or 0.3 seconds.

The New World - Colonial America

⟿ THE VIRGINIA COLONY ⟸

"Heaven and earth never agreed better to frame a place for man's habitation."
- John Smith (1607)

Truer words were never spoken. At the dawn of the 17th century the entire eastern portion of the North American continent was known as the Colony of Virginia. One-hundred-fourteen years after Columbus stumbled upon the New World in his quest for a western passage to India, the London Company petitioned the crown to grant them a charter to establish a colony in America, and in 1606 King James I consented. The Charter granted the company the right to a block of land 100-miles-square anywhere on the North American coast between the thirty-fourth and forty-first degrees of north latitude, and it wasted no time in carrying out its intention to colonize America. Captain Christopher Newport, commander of a fleet of three small ships, embarked for Virginia with a group of 105 hardy souls on December 19, 1606. He sailed into the mouth of Chesapeake Bay, formed by two projecting points of land, in the spring of 1607, naming the points Cape Henry and Cape Charles after the king's two sons. Newport then sailed about twenty-five miles up one of the wide tributaries that flowed into the bay. He named it the James River, in honor of the king, and on the north bank the group staked out their claim. Thus, the seeds of what would one day be the most powerful constitutional democracy that civilization has ever seen were sown at Jamestown, the first British settlement in the New World.

In an effort to entice Englishmen to emigrate to Virginia in the mid-1600s, a booklet was published in London which painted a rosy picture of the Virginia Colony, a "land where there is nothing wanting." It accomplished its goal, and by 1670 Virginia's population had swelled to 38,000 people.

Many trials, tribulations and disasters would be endured in the evolution from seed to seedling, and from maturity to the bearing of fruit. Famine, fever, illness and Indian massacres were commonplace during the almost 200-year journey from colony to statehood. During this period the lands claimed to be within the bounds of Virginia were expanded from the original 100-square-miles further toward the west—beyond the mountains, to the Great Lakes and to the middle of the continent, areas that now encompass the states of Illinois and Wisconsin.

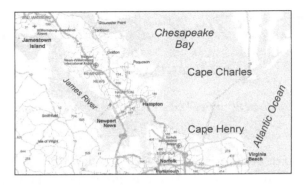

Captain Newport would barely recognize the mouth of the Chesapeake Bay today, with its multitude of bridges and tunnels.

⇒ THE MARYLAND COLONY ⇐

Two decades later, George Calvert, the first Lord Baltimore, petitioned King Charles I for a large tract of land north of the Potomac River on either side of Chesapeake Bay. In 1632 the king granted a charter for this expanse of land, soon to be known as the Province of Maryland, but Calvert died in England before he had a chance to see his charter come to fruition. His son Caecilius, the second Lord Baltimore, then inherited the grant. The borders of the new province extended from the Atlantic Ocean on the east to a meridian (a north-south line) drawn from the first spring (origin) of the Potomac River on the west. The southern boundary was to be the south bank of the Potomac and the northern border the 40th parallel of northern latitude. The grant included all of the present state of Delaware and portions of what is now Pennsylvania and West Virginia. These boundary lines immediately raised the hackles on the neck of its neighbors to the south and west, but by 1634 the heirs of Lord Baltimore had begun to colonize the territories granted by this charter.

In 1631, a year before Calvert's charter was granted, William Clayborne, a Virginia surveyor, had established an outpost on Kent Island in the Chesapeake Bay. In 1635 Lord Baltimore informed him that the island was part of the Maryland colony and was thus under his jurisdiction. With encouragement from the governor of Virginia, Clayborne defied Calvert. Soon an order for his arrest was issued, and an altercation ensued in which men from both sides lost their lives, with several Virginians being taken into custody. Clayborne eventually brought his case before the king, but his plea fell on deaf ears. Ten years later he returned and took the island by force, but his conquest was temporary. Kent

Island eventually came under the permanent control of Maryland.

To add to the confusion, the Potomac River has both a north and south branch. To which did the grant refer? If it were the south branch, many square miles of present-day West Virginia would be part of Maryland. Such ambiguities were the cause of much controversy, misunderstanding and bloodshed throughout the colonies of the New World.

Abstract from The Charter of Maryland: 1632
Provisions in respect to the boundaries

III. Know Ye therefore, that We, encouraging with our Royal Favour, the pious and noble purpose of the zaforesaid Barons of Baltimore, of our special Grace, certain knowledge, and mere Motion, have Given, Granted and Confirmed, and by this our present Charter, for Us our Heirs, and Successors, do Give, Grant and Confirm, unto the aforesaid Caecilius, now Baron of Baltimore, his Heirs, and Assigns, all that part of the Peninsula, or Chersonese, lying in the Parts of America, between the Ocean on the East and the Bay of Chesapeake on the West, divided from the Residue thereof by a Right Line drawn from the Promontory, or Head Land, called Watkin's Point, situate upon the Bay aforesaid, near the river Wigloo, on the West, unto the main Ocean on the East; and between that Boundary on the South, unto that Part of the Bay of Delaware on the North, which lieth under the Fortieth Degree of North Latitude from the Equinoctial, where New England is terminated.; And all that Tract of Land within the Metes underwritten (that is to say) passing from the said Bay, called Delaware Bay, in a right Line, by the Degree aforesaid, unto the true meridian of the first Fountain of the River Pattowmack, thence verging toward the South, unto the further Bank of the said River, and following the same on the West and South, unto a certain Place, called Cinquack, situate near the mouth of the said River, where it disembogues into the aforesaid Bay of Chesapeake, and thence by the shortest Line unto the aforesaid Promontory or Place, called Watkin's Point; so that the whole tract of land, divided by the Line aforesaid, between the main Ocean and Watkin's Point, unto the Promontory called Cape Charles, and every the Appendages thereof, may entirely remain excepted forever to Us, our Heirs and Successors.

⤙ PENN'S WOODS - PENNSYLVANIA ⤚

The story of the Mason and Dixon Line began on March 4, 1681, years before the births of the men whose name would be later associated with it. On this day King Charles II of England granted a royal charter to William Penn for land in the New World, almost five decades after Calvert received his grant, in

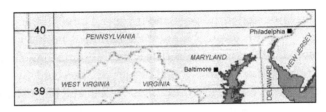

The disputed Calvert Family/Penn Family boundary between the 39th and 40th degrees of north latitude. The eventual dividing line between Maryland and Pennsylvania, located fifteen miles south of the most southern point in the City of Philadelphia, is a compromise.

order to satisfy a debt that the king owed to the Penn family. It would become known as Penn's Woods, and later Pennsylvania. The huge tract of land conveyed by this deed was to extend west five degrees in longitude from the Delaware River bounded *". . . on the South by a Circle drawn at twelve miles distance from New Castle northward and westward unto the beginning of the fortieth degree of northern latitude, and then by a straight line westward to the limit of longitude above mentioned."*

In this time period, accurate maps of the territories in the Americas were virtually non-existent. Land grants made by kings were prepared in a somewhat haphazard manner. Many of these charters—including those for the Virginia Colony, Maryland and Pennsylvania—described borders that were at best ambiguous and at worst in conflict with existing grants. In some cases, borders delineated on parchment were mathematical impossibilities in geographical terms; this was borne out when on when one attempted to actually survey those lines upon the earth.

In order to understand the politics of the times, we need to keep in mind the boundaries set forth in the original land grants. For Maryland's northern boundary: to a *". . . point which lieth under the Fortieth Degree of North Latitude from the Equinoctial."* For Pennsylvania's southern boundary: *". . . unto the beginning of the fortieth degree of Northern Latitude, and then by a straight line Westward to the Limit of Longitude above mentioned."* The *". . . point that which lieth under the Fortieth Degree of North Latitude"* would later become a bone of contention.

The legalese—once one becomes accustomed to the language and the spelling variations of the day—seemed reasonably plain. Pennsylvania was to be a province roughly bounded by three degrees of latitude and five degrees of longitude. However, the boundary between the two provinces, as written in the grants, could be interpreted differently, depending on who was doing the interpreting. As we know, the fortieth degree of north latitude was line number forty as measured north from the equator, the equator being denoted as line zero. Thus, the Calvert family's charter granted them the lands from the southern bank of the Potomac River to a point *"...which lieth under the Fortieth Degree of North Latitude..."* Taken literally, the dividing line would run straight through the present-day city of Philadelphia.

By another interpretation, a degree of latitude is the portion of physical space lying between two parallels. The distance between lines of latitude is about sixty-nine miles. The first degree of north latitude begins at the equator and ends at line number one; the second degree begins at line one and extends to line number two; and so forth. Therefore, the fortieth degree of latitude begins at line thirty-nine and ends at line forty. From this point of view, Penn's charter granted him the land between the 39th degree of latitude and the 40th degree of latitude. This interpretation places the entire present-day city of Baltimore within the bounds of Pennsylvania.

The approximately sixty-nine miles of land that lies between the 39th and 40th degree lines of north latitude, on the border between Pennsylvania and Maryland, would remain a hotly contested issue for more than eighty years. It would become difficult, and in some cases impossible, for either province to issue land patents or to collect taxes in the disputed territory. The same land would often be conveyed to two different owners in separate deeds issued by the two provinces. As a result, boundary incidents were frequent occurrences that often ended in bloodshed. The fame and fortune of many settlers would rise and fall on the issue of the border between the neighboring provinces of Pennsylvania and Maryland.

To add to the confusion, the lands that make up the present-day state of Delaware were considered part of Penn's province. They were known as the Lower Three Counties (New Castle, Kent, and Sussex). The ambiguous border between this land and the land to the west claimed by Maryland was also an issue, as was the circular border between present-day Delaware and Pennsylvania. The original royal grant for Pennsylvania specified that part of the border to be *"...a Circle drawne at twelve miles distance from New Castle Northward...."* But from where exactly in New Castle? Some individuals interjected more confusion into the conflict by claiming the twelve miles to be the circumference of the line, and not the radius. If this rendering of the charter prevailed, the actual circular border would be about three miles distant from New Castle! And so it went—on and on and on.

In 1732 the matter was brought before an English court. It was referred to the Committee for Trade and Plantations and became known as the Great Chancery Suit. Finally, in 1750—and we think the justice system is slow today—the court rendered its decision: The boundary would be a parallel of latitude fifteen miles south of the most southern point in the city of Philadelphia. This compromise was not the midpoint, as one would expect, between the 39th and 40th lines of northern latitude. In fact it gave Maryland about fifty-two of the disputed sixty-nine miles, with Pennsylvania acquiring the remaining seventeen miles.

Furthermore, the court decreed that the twelve-mile circle, mentioned previously, was to be a radius centered on the courthouse in New Castle. The southern boundary of the Lower Three Counties would be on a line of latitude that passed through Cape Henlopen. It was proposed that the border between the Lower Three Counties and the lands of Maryland would be a line drawn from the center point of this line of latitude to the tangent point on the twelve-mile circle. There was, however, still a great deal of wrangling over where and how the dividing lines would be drawn between Pennsylvania and Maryland. It was not until 1760, when a deed was agreed to by officials from both states, that the matter finally seemed to be resolved. But was it—really? The difficult part, the physical surveying and marking of the borders, still remained to be done.

Abstract from The Charter of Pennsylvania: 1681
—provisions in respect to the boundaries—

CHARLES the Second, by the Grace of God, King of England, Scotland, France and Ireland, Defender of the Faith, To all whom these presents shall come, Greets. WHEREAS Our Trustee and well beloved Subject WILLIAM PENN, Esquire, Sonne and heire of Sir WILLIAM PENN deceased, out of a commendable Desire to enlarge our English Empire, and promote such useful commodities that may bee of benefit to us and Our Dominions, as also to reduce the savage Natives by gentle and just manners to the Love of Civil Societie and Christian Religion, hath humbely besought leave of us to transport an ample Colonie unto a certaine Countrey hereinafter described in the Partes of America not yet cultivated and planted; . . . . . . In consideration thereof, of Our Speciale grace, certaine Knowledge, and meere Motion have Given and Granted, and by this Our present Charter, for Us, Our Heires and Assignes, all that Tract or Parte of Land in America, with all the Islands therein conteyned, as the same as bounded on the East by the Delaware River, from twelve miles distance Northwards of New Castle Towne unto the three and fortieth degree of Northerne Latitude, if the said River doeth extende so farre Northwards; But if said River shall not extend so farre Northward, then by the said River soe farr as it doeth extend; and from the head of the said River, the Eastern bounds are to bee determined by a meridian Line, to bee drawn from the head of the said River, unto the said three and fortieth Degree. The said Lands to extend westwards five degrees in longitude, to be computed from said Eastern Bounds; and the said Lands to be bounded on the North by the beginning of the three and fortieth degree of Northern Latitude, and on the South by a Circle drawne at twelve miles distance from New Castle Northward and Westward unto the beginning of the fortieth degree of Northern Latitude, and then by a streight line Westward to the Limit of Longitude above mentioned.

⇜ POLITICIANS & SURVEYORS ⇝

Several attempts were made by assorted public officials to initiate the work of surveying and actually marking the border. However, human nature was not much different then than it is now. In our day and age, every ten years, after the results of the census are made public, politicians of each party scramble, wheel and deal in smoke-filled rooms, engaging in all kinds of questionable negotiations and agreements to redraw the boundaries of congressional districts to their own advantage. One political party attempts to outdo the other in this game of gerrymandering—creatively drawing lines on a map carving the populace up into districts that will favor their own interests. In fact, in our time a group of Texas legislators actually left the geographic borders of the Lone Star State to prevent the gendarmes from rounding them up so that a quorum would be present to vote on redrawn legislative boundaries.

In our 18th century squabble, surveyors proposed by each party were viewed with suspicion by the other. The prevailing thought of contemporary politicians was that a surveyor from Pennsylvania would be apt to favor the Penn family; conversely, one from south of the border would be tempted to draw the line to benefit the interests of the Calverts. It is reasonable to assume that deals were being brokered in smoke-filled rooms in this era long past, as the frustrations associated with the ambiguity and lack of markings on the invisible dividing line continued between the provinces.

Agents for the Proprietors of the two colonies finally petitioned the office of the English Astronomer Royal to recommend scientists with the skills and abilities to carry out the work of surveying and marking the dividing line of north latitude. On August 4, 1763 the Proprietors of Maryland and Pennsylvania convened in London, and finalized and signed an agreement to engage the professional services of Charles Mason and Jeremiah Dixon to survey and mark the dividing lines between their respective states. In addition, each province would appoint seven commissioners to represent their interests and to supervise the work of the Englishmen.

⤙ THE CHOSEN ONES ⤚

Charles Mason was the third of four children born to Charles Mason Sr. and Anne Damsel at Wherr (now Weir) Farm, Oakridge Lynch, Gloucestershire in early 1728. He was baptized into the Anglican faith on May 1ˢᵗ of that year. The Mason family roots in the county of Gloucestershire can be traced through local church records back to the mid-1500s. Mason's early education took place in local village schools. He was befriended by Robert Stratford, a noted mathematician from a nearby village, and received additional instruction under his tutelage. At the age of twenty-eight, in 1756, Mason became an assistant to Dr. James Bradley, Astronomer Royal. As a mathematician-astronomer, he quickly ascended the ladder of success at the Royal Observatory in Greenwich, where he compiled tables of lunar distances from which one could derive the longitude of a point on the surface of the earth. Mason was known as a congenial person and a studious observer of nature and geography. He soon married and had two sons. Sadly, his beloved wife Rebekah died at the age of thirty-one in the year 1759.

Jeremiah Dixon was born into a Quaker family in Cockfield, County Durham, in 1733. He was fifth of seven children born to George Dixon and Mary Hunter. The Dixon family had lived in the area for many generations. His father was a wealthy coal mine owner. Jeremiah received his early education at John Kipling's School, Barnard Castle, where he first became interested in mathematics and astronomy, and as a young man he earned his living as a land surveyor. Later he developed a profound knowledge of mathematics, and as a result Dixon was recommended to Dr. Bradley as a prospective assistant. From what is known of him, Jeremiah was a happy-go-lucky man who possessed an impatient spirit.

Charles and Jeremiah were at opposite ends of the spectrum as far as religious convictions were concerned. Mason was a devout member of the Anglican Church, while Dixon was a disciple of the Society of Friends (Quakers). From the entries in the survey journal kept by Mason it becomes obvious that his methodology was deliberate and detailed, and that Sunday was typically observed as his day of rest. The occasional glimpse into the mind of Dixon would seem to suggest that, while he was just as talented as his partner, he preferred to look at the big picture and leave the day-to-day details to others.

In September 1760 Mason was commissioned by the Royal Society to undertake a voyage to Sumatra to observe one of the rarest of planetary alignments—the transit of Venus across the face of the sun as seen from the earth. This celestial phenomenon occurs in pairs separated by eight years, and the pairs occur at intervals of more than 100 years. Other astronomers of note were dispatched to various parts of the globe to make similar observations, in an effort to accurately determine the distance between the earth and the sun. This passing of the inner planet across the face of the sun was to occur on June 6, 1761, and it was only the third to occur since the telescope had been invented. Jeremiah Dixon was invited to be Mason's assistant, and he responded enthusiastically to the invitation. The pair began their journey from Portsmouth to the other side of the world on January 8, 1761 aboard the HMS *Seahorse*, a British fighting ship.

The voyage was not without incident. Two days out of port the *Seahorse*, barely clear of the English Channel, encountered the French privateer frigate *L'Grand*, and the two engaged in battle. By the time the war ships separated both were seriously damaged. Many members of the crew from both ships were dead, and others were seriously wounded. The *Seahorse* reversed course and headed back to Portsmouth for repairs. To say the least, the two landlubbers must have been badly shaken from the incident.

On February 3rd, Mason and Dixon hesitantly reboarded the HMS *Seahorse*. The ship sailed from Portsmouth on the flood tide that same afternoon, but the delay dashed all hopes that the scientist-astronomers would reach their intended destination in time to carry out their June 6 observations. After conferring with the captain, the pair decided to attempt their data gathering from Cape Town, South Africa, where the ship dropped anchor in late April. The observations were carried out without further incident, and they returned to England in late 1761.

Soon the pair, who had established their competence by the transit expedition, were about to confront a new challenge. The mission of the 35-year-old Charles Mason and the 30-year-old Jeremiah Dixon: Survey and mark the disputed boundaries between the lands of the Calvert family and the Penn family in the New World. An abstract from the agreement between Lord Baltimore, Thomas Penn, Richard Penn and Messrs. Mason and Dixon specified that their "*...traveling expenses and fees for the survey will be borne equally between the proprietors of the two provinces.*" It was hoped that the selection of neutral surveyors with no axe to grind would eliminate all hints of favoritism.

In the 1760s the country was still under English rule, and monetary disbursements were made in pounds, shillings and pence. For their efforts, Mason and Dixon were to be paid on a per diem basis—one pound, one shilling for each day they spent in America. In 21st century U.S. currency, this is the equivalent of about $129, or approximately $47,000 a year for each man. However, the survey nore than just a twosome. Payroll records indicate that at one point, ... the survey was nearing its end, there were as many as 115 workers employed. Job descriptions ranged from axe man, cook, waggoner and tent keeper to guides, chain carrier and butcher. During the later part of the summer of 1767, fourteen Indians from the Six Nations Confederation, under the direction of an interpreter, joined the group to offer some protection against hostile Indians. Wages for workers ranged from a little over $100 a week to somewhat over $200 a week. Labor and other expenses probably brought the total bill for the survey to well over $5,000,000. This cost was equally shared between the Penns and the Calverts—the Proprietors of the provinces—as per their agreement.

On Saturday morning, September 3, 1763, Charles Mason and Jeremiah Dixon boarded the packet boat with their baggage and instruments. At high tide the ship departed Falmouth for America. In the wildest of their dreams they could not have imagined the adventure that they were about to undertake.

➤ TUESDAY - NOVEMBER 15, 1763 ➤

As Mason and Dixon sailed up the Delaware River toward Philadelphia they were venturing through a region where a plethora of history had preceded them. They were also entering a land that was about to experience an explosion of events, a country rife with labor pains; a land about to give birth to a nation that one day would become the most powerful the planet has ever experienced.

More than a century prior to their voyage, at the site of present-day Wilmington, Delaware, the Swedes had colonized the territory where the Christiana River empties into the Delaware. A few miles further up the river they would have passed Tinicum Island, where Governor Johan Prinz had established his capital of New Sweden in 1638.

Their route took them within about five miles of where I first entered the world as a newborn some 177 years later. As a youngster, my parents frequently took the family to a site that overlooks the Delaware—Red Bank Battlefield Park was just a few minutes drive from our home in Woodbury. We all called it "the monument," a nickname derived from the 75-foot white stone marker that had been erected in the park at the beginning of the 20th century. The memorial is a reminder of the price paid by our forefathers in their 18th century quest for freedom and independence.

Located on the New Jersey side of the Delaware, the park is directly across that waterway from the mouth of the Schuylkill River. It is the site of old

The monument – focal point of the Red Bank Battlefield (l). The restored James and Ann Whitall House (r).

Fort Mercer, named for Brigadier General Hugh Mercer, who fell at the Battle of Princeton. The structure was built for the defense of Philadelphia during the Revolutionary War, and the Battle of Red Bank was fought here in October 1777. Still standing in the park, and handsomely restored to its original 18th century elegance, is the James and Ann Whitall House. The structure was built in 1748 and served as the center of activity on the 400-acre Whitall Plantation for 114 years. During the battle the house was pressed into service as a military hospital.

It is a blustery autumn afternoon. Standing in the park on a bluff about 100 feet above the water, I gaze to the south. From this vantage point one is afforded a commanding view of the river channel approach to Philadelphia. I am practicing the age-old art of daydreaming, recalling many fond memories of years past that took place on or near this spot. As a youngster, at waters edge, I tossed numerous flat stones in an effort to skip them across the water. Standing on almost this same spot, as a young teenager, I drowned worms on a fishing hook on many summer afternoons. Mom claimed I was wasting my time—surely no fish could survive in the polluted waters of the Delaware River. But one day I proved her wrong when I reeled in a catfish that was almost three feet long—a prize catch for a thirteen-year-old! Later, as a young man, I proudly captained my own craft, an 18-foot fiberglass boat, up and down the river, and into every tributary that was deep enough for exploration. I had learned to water ski behind that boat on the broad surface of the mile-wide river that divided two states. Somehow I escaped another one of mom's predictions: "If you keep swimming in that river you'll surely come down with one of those exotic waterborne diseases harbored in that polluted waterway." This place holds many memories of happy days gone by.

Suddenly, I am jolted back to present-day consciousness. There is an ocean-going container ship coming toward me, making its way up the forty-foot-deep dredged channel of the river. Its obvious destination is the Port of Philadelphia, where it will disgorge its cargo of imported goods. Serving as a backdrop for the ship is a massive jet airliner descending from the clouds on its approach over Tinicum Island onto runway 9R at Philadelphia International Airport. Originally swampland, the area was once home to the short-lived privately owned Hog Island Shipyard. The complex was expeditiously built in 1917 to address a dire shortage of cargo ships and troop carriers as the United States was swept into World War I. The next year, the first of the 121 seventy-five-hundred-ton ships that would follow slid down its ways into the river. Just to the north, at the confluence of the Schuylkill and Delaware, is League Island. It was the home of the Philadelphia Navy Yard for just shy of 200 years. In 1799 Congress appropriated a little over half-a-million dollars to acquire the original plot of land for the shipyard. In 1996 it ceased operation as a government owned entity, and today it is home to a privately owned business that constructs container ships and tankers. The Navy now stores decommissioned and mothballed war ships in a sheltered basin which was once part of the shipyard.

After a few moments my mind wandered even farther into the past—far beyond the days of my youth. I imagined that I was standing there, on that spot, on a Tuesday afternoon, more than two hundred years ago—November 15, 1763 to be exact. The ship I was watching come up the channel was a two-masted packet ship—a vessel flying the British Union Jack. In addition to its human cargo, it carried mail and small cargo items from the British Isles to various ports of call in the Americas. The ship, under full sail, was headed for the bustling port of Philadelphia. The passenger manifest included the names of Charles Mason and Jeremiah Dixon, who, along with the other passengers, had not set foot on dry land for several weeks. All were standing on the deck, waiting in anxious anticipation of being sprung from their self-imposed captivity on a small wooden sailing ship that had just crossed 3000 miles across the tumultuous North Atlantic Ocean. Perhaps James and Ann Whitall were watching them from the bluff beside their house, standing on the exact same spot where I was standing! The Whitalls and passengers may even have waved to each other as the ship made its way north.

The cargo manifest that day included a zenith sector, and other delicate instruments, which would enable Mason and Dixon to carry out their commission to settle the long-standing boundary dispute between the Penn and Calvert families. At this point the two Englishmen must have been keen to shed their

The Delaware River—gateway to the New World.

sea legs and set foot on solid ground after their ten-week voyage.

This spot on the bank of the Delaware has been personal witness to decades of history. By the time of the surveyor's arrival, the relationship between the colonists and the crown was quickly deteriorating, and the seeds of revolution were beginning to sprout. This area of the New World provided fertile ground for the growth of this unrest.

With the gift of clairvoyance and a crystal ball, one could have easily foreseen the events of the next decade: The Sons of Liberty breaking open the tea chests of the East India Company and tossing their contents into Boston Harbor; British retaliation by the closing of the port of Boston by Parliament; the first gathering of the Continental Congress; and the act that finally cut the umbilical cord—the signing of the Declaration of Independence in Philadelphia in 1776.

In September 1777 the British would occupy Philadelphia. Fort Mercer and Fort Mifflin (located on Mud Island on the Pennsylvania side of the river) would quickly become a thorn in the side of King George III's army. The Patriots who occupied these forts would have a detrimental effect on British shipping on the river. They launched several marine chevaux-de-frise—devices constructed from six timbers the diameter of utility poles—into the waterway. Designed so that three poles protruded upward just a few degrees from the vertical, they were tipped with sharp iron spikes. The chevaux were assembled into huge thirty by forty-foot boxes, each weighted down with thirty tons of stone. The entire contrivance was then floated out into the river channel and plugs were pulled from the bottom of the boxes to force them to flood and sink. When the weighted box then settled to the bottom, the tops of the iron-spiked timbers, facing downstream and tilted at about a five-degree angle, were but a few feet below the surface of the water at ebb tide. A massive iron chain connected several chevaux together, making them difficult to remove. As unwitting British war ships and supply ships sailed over the submerged spikes, the bottoms of their wooden hulls were torn open and they were either severely damaged or sunk.

General Howe, the Commander-in-Chief of British Forces in America, dispatched three battalions of Hessian troops in an effort to eliminate the source of the disruption. The Patriots, under Colonel Christopher Greene, Commandant of Fort Mercer, inflicted more than 600 fatalities on the Hessians. Green's losses amounted to less than 50 men. During the battle the HMS *Augusta* opened fire on the fort, and one of its cannonballs tore through the wall of the Whitall House. The next day the warship ran aground, and the colonists set it afire. Flames quickly reached the powder storage area, and more than 100 British sailors died in the enormous explosion that followed.

Indeed, this is hallowed ground. Within sight and within earshot of the 18th century Fort Mercer cannon on which I was now leaning, just a hundred yards or so from the Whitall House, the seeds of the new nation had been sowed. This house was the first sign of civilization in the New World on which Mason and Dixon set sight.

⊷ WILLIAM PENN'S CITY ⊷

TUESDAY - NOVEMBER 15, 1763
"Arrived at Philadelphia"

King Charles II owed a substantial amount of money—16,000 pounds sterling—about $22,000—to the Penn family. In 1681, William Senior, the patriarch, accepted a large portion of land as payment for the debt—land bounded on the east by the Delaware River, on the west by a meridian of west longitude drawn five degrees in distance from the eastern boundary, on the south by the soon-to-be-measured parallel of latitude that lies fifteen miles south of Philadelphia, and on the north by the 42nd parallel of north latitude. With the later addition of a small piece of land in its northwest corner, Penn's province was approximately 44,892 square miles in size. Before the elder Penn could make arrangements to visit his colony he died, and the grant passed to his son William. In 1682 he received the charter for the province, situated between New York to the north and Maryland to the south. Among his proposed list of names for the colony were "New Wales" and "Sylvania"—the latter meaning "abounding in woods." The king, however, came forward and insisted that it be named in honor of the elder Penn. In an effort to accommodate the king's wishes the son compromised, and Pennsylvania— Penn's Woods—was born. In the late summer of 1662, the new proprietor of this vast expanse of unexplored land boarded the sailing vessel HMS *Welcome* and set out to visit his province in the New World. Shortly after the ship dropped anchor near the western bank of the Delaware, Penn envisioned a "green country town", and he immediately took a hands-on role in the planning and layout of the city of Philadelphia.

Larger than life, from atop City Hall, Billy Penn watches over his beloved City of Philadelphia.

Although born into a Quaker family, William did not seriously embrace the practice of his religion until he was in his 20s. He was a man of peace and benevolence, and it is not surprising that one of his first official acts as Proprietor was to sign a treaty with the Lenni Lenape Indians. He also made payment to them for encroaching on their lands. "I desire to gain your love and friendship, by a kind, just and peaceable life" he told the chief of the tribe. His city, Philadelphia, became known as the "City of Brotherly Love."

William, affectionately known to his friends as Billy, became disabled in 1712 due to an apparent brain aneurysm. His second wife, Hannah, managed his affairs until he died in 1718. Upon her death in 1727, proprietorship of the colony passed to Penn's three sons—John, Thomas and Richard.

In 1763, Philadelphia occupied only a fraction of the land area that it encompasses today. It was about 1200 acres in size, with borders extending from the Delaware River on the east to the Schuylkill River on the west. The southern limit of the city was South Street, then known as Cedar Street. The northern boundary was present-day Vine Street. When Mason and Dixon walked down the gangway of the ship and set foot on the dock, Philadelphia was the second largest city, in population, in the British Empire. Even at that early date it had made its mark as a busy port city. The center of its economy was the exportation of raw materials and grain. A quarter century later it would briefly become the capital city of a new nation formed from the thirteen original British colonies.

Philadelphia sits on the west bank of the 390-mile long Delaware River, approximately sixty miles inland from the Atlantic Ocean. Today, at the dawn of the 21ˢᵗ century, the river provides a path for the 3000 ocean-going ships that come and go from the port every year. About forty-four million tons of cargo are loaded and off-loaded annually, and the city's airport serves more than twenty-four million passengers each year. Philadelphia is the fifth largest city in the United States, boasting a population of more than one-and-a-half million people. Its metropolitan area is home to more than six million people.

A little more than a decade before Mason and Dixon set foot in Philadelphia the city had become home to another famous visitor from England— albeit it one that was inanimate in nature. In 1751, in commemoration of the 50ᵗʰ anniversary of the proclamation of William Penn's Charter of Privileges— Pennsylvania's original Constitution—London's Whitechapel Bell Foundry was commissioned to cast a 2000-pound bronze bell. On it were inscribed the words "By order of the Assembly of the Province of Pennsylvania for the State House in the City of Philadelphia". It arrived on the ship *Hibernia* some ten months later, and was duly hung in the belfry of the State House, the building that would later become known as Independence Hall. To the horror of all those who had gathered for the initial ringing of the bell, it cracked when struck by the clapper. The bell was recast, not just once but on several occasions, to repair flaws, in an effort to improve its flat sounding ring.

The State House bell was tolled to summon the people together for special events, such as when Benjamin Franklin was sent to the mother country to address Colonial grievances and the gathering of the First Continental Congress. On July 8, 1776 it was used to summon the people together for the reading of the Declaration of Independence after it was hammered out by the Second Continental Congress. A few months before the British Army occupied Philadelphia in 1777, all large bells were removed from the city. There were well-founded fears that if they fell into the hands of the British army they would be melted down and used to make cannon balls. The State House bell was carted off to Allentown and hidden in the basement of the Zion Reformed Church. In 1839 this great symbol of American independence and liberty was renamed the Liberty Bell, and is today owned by the City of Philadelphia. It can be viewed twenty-four hours a day in the brand new Liberty Bell Center in the downtown area of the city.

WEDNESDAY - NOVEMBER 16, 1763
"Attended a meeting of the Commissioners appointed by the Proprietors of Pennsylvania to settle the boundaries of the Province"

The proprietors of the two provinces—the Penns and the Calverts—each had appointed seven agents or commissioners to represent their interests during the survey and marking of the great dividing line. The enthusiasm of the newly arrived Englishmen was evident by the early activities recorded in their journal. The pair wasted no time in getting started on their assignment. Within twenty-four hours of setting foot in Philadelphia, they met with the representatives from Pennsylvania to announce their arrival.

THURSDAY - NOVEMBER 17, 1763
"Wrote to his Excellency Horatio Sharpe, Esquire, Governor of Maryland, signifying our arrival at Philadelphia"

In an obvious effort to avoid the appearance of favoritism toward the Penns, Mason penned a letter the next day to the Honorable Horatio Sharp, the Governor of Maryland, informing him of their arrival.

⇠ EIGHTEENTH CENTURY SURVEYOR'S TOOLS ⇢

TUESDAY - NOVEMBER 22, 1763
"Landed the instruments"

The zenith telescope or zenith sector was by far the most delicate of the instruments the pair brought along from England. It was a basic instrument of astronomy and geodesy, a refracting telescope designed to measure the angle between the zenith—the point directly overhead of the observer—and a star as it crosses the meridian—the point directly north or south of the observer. Robert Hooke is credited with being the inventor of this instrument, in 1669, when he used it in his efforts to discover evidence of the earth's annual motion about the sun.

Prior to the signing on of Mason and Dixon, but confident of eventually finding and engaging the services of competent and unbiased surveyors agreeable to the Calverts for the survey, Thomas Penn commissioned John Bird, a Fellow of the Royal Society of Astronomers, to produce an improved version of the zenith telescope or zenith sector. By observing the position of the stars in the heavens through this instrument, a determination of the observer's latitude could be made. The final design was built around a tube six feet in length through which a plumb line was adjusted to bisect a point in the center of the instrument. The tube was mounted so that it was capable of rotating on both its vertical and horizontal axis. It was set upon a tripod so that when the plumb line was centered the tube was pointed directly vertical. The cross hairs at the far end of the tube bisected a point in the sky that was directly overhead. By the use of an adjustment knob called a tangent micrometer screw, graduated in seconds of arc, the center of the cross hairs could be adjusted to measure the deviation of a star from the zenith, in degrees, minutes and seconds, when it passed directly north or south of the observer. Zenith sectors, with tube lengths of twenty-five feet, mounted in observatories on stone foundations for added stability, had reported accuracies within 0.1 seconds of arc, which translates to about ten feet on the ground. The accuracy of the portable device Mason and Dixon brought on their 3000 mile journey across the North Atlantic was about ±3 seconds of arc—about 300 feet on the ground. The instrument had been packed carefully so as to minimize the possibility of damage during its ten week journey across the choppy sea.

Eighteenth Century Surveyor's Measuring Units

GUNTER'S CHAIN
1 link = 0.66 feet = 7.92 inches
1 chain = 22 yards = 66 feet = 100 links
80 chains = 1 mile = 5280 feet

THE SURVEYOR'S LEVEL
1 level = 16.5 feet

In addition to the zenith sector, the survey party utilized several other tools of the trade. In 1620, Edmund Gunter introduced a 66-foot chain, containing 100 links, for measuring horizontal distances. Mason and Dixon used the Gunter's Chain for measurements across level ground. Subsequently, all of the distances in their journal were recorded in miles (5280 feet), chains (66 feet) and links (7.92 inches).

A measurement with the chain up one side of a mountain and then down the other side would yield a measurement longer than the actual flat horizontal stretch between the two points. Surveyor's levels, 16.5 feet in length, were used to measure linear distance when the line took them up and over hills and mountains. Two or more men positioned the level, using a plumb-bob, at the end of the last level measurement. The device was kept perfectly horizontal—thus the term level—and its forward edge, again using the plumb-bob, was marked on the ground. The operation was then repeated. The resultant measurement was not unlike gauging the horizontal distance traversed by a stairway by measuring only the width of the individual stair treads while disregarding the risers.

Besides the sector, the levels, and the Gunter's Chain, other instruments unloaded from the ship included two transits and two reflecting telescopes. These would enable them to observe posts in the line for a distance of ten to twelve miles. Each was carefully inspected for damage, but luckily none was apparent.

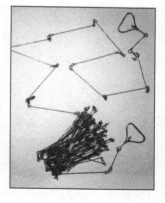

⇥ THE OBSERVATORY ON CEDAR STREET ⇤

An 18th century Gunter's Chain, used by surveyors to record distance in miles, chains and links.

TUESDAY - DECEMBER 5, 1763
"Attended a meeting of the Commissioners and directed a carpenter to build an observatory near the point settled by the Commissioners to be the South end of the City of Philadelphia"

One point on which all of the parties—those that represented the Penns and those that represented the Calverts—seemed to agree on was that the north wall of a particular house—the home of Thomas Plumbstead and Joseph Huddle on the south west corner of Cedar Street and Second Street—was the southernmost point in the city of Philadelphia in 1763. The point at the northwest corner of the intersection of what is today Second Street and South Street, not far from the Delaware River, is where Mason and Dixon set up their observatory. Accurate determination of latitude typically required from ten to fourteen clear nights of stellar observations. The pair enlisted the services of a carpenter to build a shelter, and the refuge was quickly fabricated from wood and canvas. It would soon offer the men and their instruments protection from the harsh weather that Mother Nature was about to thrust upon them. The actual location of the observatory was about 120 feet—1.2 seconds of latitude—north of the agreed upon point. This offset would be taken into account during the ensuing observations and calculations.

On December 6th Mason and Dixon took an oath before the commissioners to officially carry out their mandate to survey and mark the border that had caused so much contention during the past eighty years. The

The area around 2nd and Cedar Streets (now South Street) as it appears in the 21st century.

observatory was completed on the 10th, and the pair set up their instruments over the next few days. Finally, they were ready for the serious business of stargazing, but the weatherman has other ideas. From their journal entry it appears that completion of their observatory occurred just in the nick of time.

WEDNESDAY - THURSDAY - DECEMBER 14 AND 15, 1763
"Rain and Snow"

FRIDAY - DECEMBER 16, 1763
"Brought the Instrument into the Meridian by making several stars pass along the horizontal wire in the middle of the Telescope"

At last, on Friday the 16th, in the damp chill of mid-December, stargazing commenced. The immediate task was to make enough stellar observations to compute their exact position of north latitude for the eighteenth century high-tech observatory. Due to their training and experience, both men were well aware that accuracy was of the utmost importance. It would be from this position that the line of true latitude, fifteen miles due south, would be reckoned and marked.

The distance to the stars is so vast that the annual motion of the earth around the sun has no observable effect on their relative positions in the sky. The 24-hour rotation of the earth on its axis is the reason that the stars appear to move across the celestial sphere. From any vantage point on the surface of the earth, these heavenly bodies appear to rise in the east, reach their peak altitude when they are on the meridian, i.e., directly north or south of the observer, then move on to set in the west. If a star reaches its maximum altitude, or peak in the sky, at 35 degrees above the north or south horizon this evening, if observed from the same spot on the earth, it will peak at 35 degrees tomorrow, 35 degrees a month from now, and at 35 degrees every night—or day—of the year. The surveyors possessed star tables that had been prepared by the Royal Observatory in London. These tables—or almanacs—were commonly used by mariners to determine their latitude while at sea. They listed the declination of a multitude of stars in degrees, minutes and seconds. If you were located at a spot on the earth at the latitude of the star's declination, it would peak at the zenith, or point directly overhead. For example, if a star has a declination of 40 degrees, and your observation point was in the city of Philadelphia, directly on the 40th degree of latitude, when the star was at its highest point in the sky it would be directly overhead. If you observed this same star from a point in College Park, Maryland, at its highest point in the sky it would appear to be 1 degree north of the zenith. Thus, by subtracting one degree from the star's known declination of 40 degrees you would have determined that College Park, Maryland is at latitude of 39 degrees.

Clouds precluded any observations on Saturday night, and Sunday was set aside as a day of rest. Monday evening, the 19th, brought clear skies, so surveillance of the northern sky through the zenith sector began in earnest. The zenith sector used for the observations was equipped with a micrometer. It would be used to determine the angle north or south of the zenith when the star crossed the meridian.

The exactness of the determination of the latitude of this point was paramount in the men's minds. Even a minor error here would negate the precision of every other point surveyed during their upcoming four-year enterprise in America; thus, the entire marking of the border was firmly tied to this one observation. More than a hundred celestial measurements of the position of seven individual stars were carefully observed, and their exact position north or south of the zenith was noted as they crossed the meridian night after night. Observations took place over a period spanning seventeen nights. On January 4th they arrived at a mean value of latitude as given by five stars: Beta Aurigae, Castor, Cygni, Alpha Lyrae and Delta Persei. The results of these observations, and all subsequent ones, were averaged to minimize error.

SATURDAY - DECEMBER 31, 1763

". ... the mean of the latitudes given by the five different stars at the observatory is equal to 39 degrees 56 minutes 30.2 seconds. The southern most point in the city of Philadelphia is south of this point (by) 1.1 seconds. True latitude of the Southernmost point of the City of Philadelphia is 39° 56' 29.1".

Observations and measurements with 21st century state-of-the-art technology indicate agreement to within two-and-a-half seconds—about 250 feet.

WEDNESDAY - JANUARY 4, 1764
"Finished our observations at Philadelphia"

If an attempt was made to measure due south from this point, the 15-mile line would cut diagonally across the Delaware River into the dense Pine Barrens of southern New Jersey. From there, at the 15-mile point, the line would have to be surveyed to the west, across part of New Jersey, and then back across the Delaware. The river was more than a mile wide at these points, so a diagonal cut would be a mile-and-a-half or more across water. Such a measurement was not an impossibility, but there were more practical and less time-consuming ways of accomplishing the same end. As a result, it had been previously decided that it would be more expedient to move to a point of equal latitude to the west of the one measured in Philadelphia.

⚬ JOHN HARLAND'S FARM ⚬

SATURDAY - JANUARY 7, 1764
"Set out from Philadelphia with a Quadrant to find (nearby) a place in the Forks of Brandywine having the same Parallel as the Southernmost point of the City of Philadelphia."

SUNDAY - JANUARY 8, 1764
"Fixed on the house of Mr. John Harland's (about 31 miles West of Philadelphia) to bring our instruments to."

Imagine the surprise of the Harlands. Knock-knock! "Hello - I am Charles Mason from Gloucestershire, England. I, and my colleague Jeremiah Dixon, have been commissioned by the Penns and the Calverts to survey and mark the border between the provinces of Pennsylvania and Maryland. We have chosen your garden for our pivot point. We will be spending a great deal of time here in and around your neighborhood over the next three years!" The initial visit of the Englishmen might not have come as a total surprise to John and his family. There is some evidence that others used this very point more than twenty-five years

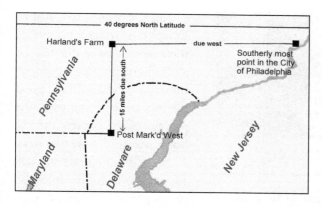

The positioning of THE POST MARK'D WEST fifteen miles south of the most southerly point in the city of Philadelphia, circa 1763.

prior to their visit in an unsuccessful attempt to accomplish the same ends that Mason and Dixon were pursuing.

The Harland farm is in the present-day town of Embreeville, Pennsylvania. Its exact distance west of the original point in Philadelphia was not important, but determination of its exact position of latitude was of extreme importance. The accuracy of the location of the Maryland-Pennsylvania border would depend entirely on the diligence with which observations at this point were made.

Monday - January 9, 1764
"Returned to Philadelphia"

Wednesday - January 11, 1764
"The observatory taken down and put with the rest of our instruments into the wagons, except the Telescope, etc, of the sector which was carried on the Springs (with the feather bed under it) of a single Horse chair."

Twenty-first century travelers have little appreciation for the trials and tribulations of making a thirty-one mile trip in 1764. With modern transportation and paved highways, such a trip is at most less than an hour long. I left downtown Philadelphia at 9:30 a.m. drove the Schuylkill Expressway to Valley Forge, took the Pennsylvania Turnpike to Downingtown, and then followed back roads to Harland's Farm, arriving at 10:20 a.m. At best, roads in 1764 were unpaved trails or footpaths, and in the month of January one could optimistically expect the ground to be frozen and devoid of mud. However, if lady luck was not a traveling companion, there could be a foot or more of snow covering the trail, making it difficult to track and follow. The typical Eastern Pennsylvania January mid-winter freeze-and-thaw could produce a trail of soft, wet muck that was unfriendly

Ye Olde Mill at Embreeville sits on the banks of Brandywine Creek at the dawn of the 21ˢᵗ century.

to any horse and wagon. From the apparent ease of their travel, as indicated by journal entries, conditions on the trail were probably good for this time of the year. The journey of the convoy and the horsemen took only two days.

The preferred method of transport in the mid-18th century was by horse. Absent the horse it was by foot power! The party's fragile equipment was packed and carried in specially constructed, padded cases. The zenith sector was the bread-and-butter of the survey effort—without it, the surveyors were out of business—so a delicate instrument such as this merited a featherbed on a horse chair equipped with springs. The rest of the equipment was stowed in three horse-drawn covered wagons.

SATURDAY - JANUARY 14, 1764

"Arrived at Mr. Harland's and set up the sector in his Garden (enclosed in a tent), and in the evening brought the instrument into the Meridian, and took the following observations . . ."

The next forty-four days—until February 28th—were spent stargazing during every clear night. Daylight hours were reserved for the laborious calculations needed to determine their position of north latitude. Mason's notes indicate that the observatory in John Harland's garden was at north latitude 39 degrees, 56 minutes, 18.9 seconds. This was 11.3 seconds, or a little more than eleven hundred feet, south of their observation point on Cedar Street in Philadelphia.

As per their contract, Mason and Dixon were required to place blocks of limestone quarried in southern England at one-mile intervals, each weighing several hundred pounds. At every fifth mile, these stones (called Crownstones) were engraved with the Penn and Calvert coat-of-arms—the Penn coat facing the Pennsylvania side, and the Calvert facing Maryland.

My determination of the location of their first marker stone—called the Star Gazer Stone—is based on the observation of twenty-four man-made stars on a bright spring morning. It took the eighteenth century surveyors more than a month of observation and calculation to determine their position. My GPS receiver quickly locks on to the NAVSTAR satellites, and within minutes confirms the accuracy of their calculations of north latitude to within one hundred feet.

A map of Newlin Township, Pennsylvania, as divided, dated April 1730, identifies a 125-acre plot of land owned by George Harland. The Harland family were Quakers who settled in eastern Pennsylvania in 1687. Their farm, close to the forks of Brandywine Creek, passed from George to his eldest son John in the mid-1700s, and he, his wife and five children lived in the stone farmhouse on the plot. This farm would become the point where the surveyor's efforts would turn from due west to due south to determine where the dividing line of latitude between Pennsylvania and Maryland would be located.

This part of Pennsylvania, located in the rolling hills of Chester County, sports some magnificent scenery. The population of Newlin Township today is just a bit over 1000, and the countryside is still very rustic, with forests intermingling with small farms. Within a mile of Harland's garden is an old mill, perched on the bank of the Brandywine. For the most part, with the exception of the asphalt-paved roads and a few more houses, the area probably appears today much as it did when the survey party hauled Gunter's Chains, surveyor's levels and the zenith sector through it more than two centuries ago.

The site of Harland's farmhouse is at the intersection of Embreeville Road (PA Route 162) and (appropriately named) Stargazers Road. The 17th century dwelling still stands on the northeast corner of this intersection. You have to look carefully—I missed it the first time I visited the area. While the house is within twenty-five feet of the intersection, huge yews and a hedge effectively hide it from view. During my visit, there is a car parked in the driveway behind the house, and several windows are open for ventilation. I knock on the door, just as Mason must have done more than two centuries past, and immediately hear footsteps. My adrenaline level rises. A woman's head pops out of the door, and I introduce myself and inform her of my mission.

"Is this the old Harland Farmhouse?" I ask. "It sure is!" she replies. I tell her of my mission. "Could I talk with you for a minute or two?"

I am invited inside. Kate Roby, the 21st century proprietor of the farmhouse, shares with me some of the information she has collected over the years about the farm and the Harland Family. The house was owned by descendents of John Harland until 1950, and she is only the second non-family owner. She purchased it in 1983, without any prior knowledge of its place in American history. It was only later that she discovered that it once housed two famous surveyors.

"I was looking for an old farmhouse," she said, "And I fell in love with

The 18th century Harland family farmhouse.

this one." I agree with her decision.

The original part of the house was built in the 1690s, with several additions added over the years. Kate graciously gave me a tour of the lower level of the old-fashioned Colonial dwelling. I felt goose bumps as I stood in front of the walk-in fireplace in the same spot where the Englishmen probably kicked off their boots and enjoyed the warmth of a roaring fire during the long Pennsylvania winter.

The British surveyors obviously hit it off well with the Harlands. The pair spent a good deal of their leisure time during the survey at the Harland farm, and during the next several years it would become their winter headquarters. Were they just naturally likable chaps, or is there more to the story? Kate has studied the genealogy of the Harland Family in an effort to answer this question. John Harland's grandmother was Dinah Dixon, who came from Yorkshire, Jeremiah's home county! Was this sheer coincidence or were the winter quarters for the surveyors arranged in advance through family ties? We may never know the answer.

Kate shows me a copy of a handwritten license, written by a magistrate in the employ of the Penn Family. Issued for a period of four years to John Harland in 1750, it authorized the operation of "*a publick house for entertainment and accommodations*", otherwise known as a tavern. It was located somewhere on the property but no one is certain of its exact location.

John Harland's name also appears in the survey's payroll records for the month of April 1764. With his local knowledge, he apparently picked up some pocket money before spring planting time by helping the surveyors cut their way through the heavily wooded countryside of Chester and New Castle counties.

Mason and Dixon would today search in vain for Harland's garden. The 21st century location of their 18th century pivot point is due north of the farmhouse, along Stargazer Road, in the corner of the neatly manicured front lawn of a million-dollar mansion. I was expecting too much by looking for an historical marker along the road. Kate tells me that there is a marker on Stargazers Road next to a set of overgrown stairs. In addition, there was another on Route 162 that disappeared about fifteen years ago when the Pennsylvania Department of Transportation performed shoulder work on the road.

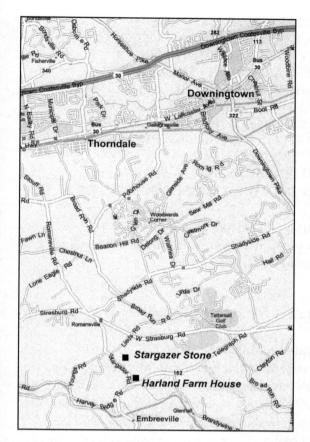

The location of the Harland farmhouse and the Stargazer Stone at the intersection of PA Route 162 and Stargazer Road in Embreeville, Pennsylvania.

My GPS receiver indicates that I am within 150 feet of the stone, but it is nowhere to be seen. There is an open-top stone enclosure, about two feet tall and five feet square, not more than 75 feet north of the driveway entrance to the mansion, evidently on private property. I get out of the car and walk over to it, at every step expecting to be challenged by either the sheriff or a Doberman, but today there is nary a soul in sight. (Kate later told me that the Chester County Historical Society owns the postage stamp size plot on which the stone resides, as well as the narrow right-of-way leading up to it. The Chester County Historical Society erected the protective enclosure in 1908.) Sitting prominently in the middle is the weather-beaten quartzite stone planted in the 18th century to mark the spot where the great survey switched direction from west to south. It is not certain that Mason and Dixon installed this stone, although the brass plaque on the protective wall states that they did. Local historians think that others may have placed it there during an earlier 1736 attempt to mark the same boundary. What all agree upon, however, is that Mason and Dixon used the marker as their pivot point, and that their observatory shelter was set in place above the stone. The plaque tells the story of the two-and-a-half century old quartz monument:

THE STAR-GAZER'S STONE
ERECTED IN 1764 BY MASON AND DIXON
IN LOCATING THE
PENNSYLVANIA-MARYLAND BOUNDARY LINE
BEING 15 MILES DUE WEST OF PHILADELPHIA. HERE
THEY ALSO MEASURED A DEGREE OF LATITUDE
ON THE EARTH'S SURFACE SOUTHWARD AND
MADE OTHER ASTRONOMICAL OBSERVATIONS.
HENCE THE NAME.
ENCLOSED AND MARKED BY
THE CHESTER COUNTY HISTORICAL SOCIETY 1908

SATURDAY - FEBRUARY 28, 1764

*"Finished our observations of the star's Zenith Distances at Mr. Harland's
in the Forks of the Brandywine."*

➤ FIFTEEN MILES SOUTH ➤

SATURDAY - MARCH 17, 1764

*"Employed one man, cutting a visto Meridian Southward. This evening at 8h 21m
9s apparent time the Eclipse of the Moon ended. The edge of the Sun's shadow [Mason
no doubt meant "Earth's shadow"] on the Moon's disk was the best defined that I ever
saw, the air was so clear it was remarkably distinct from the penumbral shape."*
[A penumbra is an area of partial darkness around a completely dark area.]

The weather was cloudy every night for almost two weeks. To add to
the late winter misery, there was also rain and snow, which stopped just in time
for Mason to observe an eclipse of the moon on the 17th of the month. On that
same day he and his partner begin the process of employing the hired hands that
would make up the survey party. The first of the laborers was dispatched to begin
cutting a path through the forest to the south. Within a few days, the group
consisted of five hired hands.

MONDAY - APRIL 2, 1764

"Began to measure from our observatory (at Mr. Harland's). Employed five men."

April 2nd marked the beginning of the effort to measure a line for a
distance of fifteen miles south through the dense forests of Chester County,

The Stargazer Stone sits in a protective wall erected by the Chester County Historical Society.

Pennsylvania into present-day New Castle County, Delaware. The tools used for this part of the mission were the 66-foot-long Gunter's Chain, where the ground was level, and the 16 1/2-foot frames—surveyor's levels—when their route took them over the small hills that dot the southeastern Pennsylvania countryside. The surveyors' journal recorded distance in miles, chains and links; to assure accuracy, all distances were measured twice, and some portions were measured three times.

On Wednesday, April 4, 1764 the crew passed close to the present-day junction of Embreeville Road and Doe Run Road (PA Route 82 and PA Route 162) in Unionville. Had they been but two and a third centuries later I would have invited them to join me for lunch in the nearby country store, a charming turn-of-the-century stone building which sits on the northeastern corner of the intersection. They could have enjoyed of some of the scrumptious nourishment available in the little deli—the turkey sandwich and handful of homemade potato chips which I consume on this 21st century Wednesday are provisions fit for the palate of a king!

The men continued cutting their way south through the woodlands for another week. The following Thursday, April 12th, the point fifteen miles south of Philadelphia was established in a farm field owned by Alexander Bryan. It was about three miles east of what is today the western boundary of Delaware. Their calculations indicated that they were too far south by about 220 feet, so the point was moved back 2 chains, 93 links to the north.

For the next eight weeks Mason and Dixon refined their measurement of the fifteen miles, and calculate the exact latitude of the point ultimately established in Mr. Bryan's field.

➤ THE POST MARK'D WEST ➤

TUESDAY - JUNE 12, 1764

"The Point 15 miles South of the Southernmost Point of the City of Philadelphia is situated in Mill Creek Hundred in the County of New Castle, in a Plantation belonging to Mr. Alexander Bryan. The Middle of the Front of Mr. Bryans house, bears from the point 37 degrees 52 seconds Northwesterly distant 23.38 chains. From the Point to the middle of a small rivulet Called Muddy Run, on a due South course is 7.15 chains."

At this place, the crew installed an important white-painted oak survey marker post. Carved into its western face was the word **WEST**. It was designated in the survey journal as **The Post Mark'd West**. This marker would serve as the base point from which all other measurements would be reckoned in miles, chains and links on the parallel of latitude soon to form the southern boundary of Pennsylvania. An average value of north latitude calculated from their numerous star observations indicated that the Post Mark'd West was at N 39 degrees 43 minutes 18.2 seconds.

For any serious student of the Mason Dixon Line, a visit to the Post Mark'd West—the anchor point of the east-west line—is a must. Its location is not well publicized; there are no signs stating "This way to the most famous survey marker ever planted in the United States!"

I carefully calculate the approximate location of the post and mark it on a 7.5 minute USGS Newark East Quadrangle typographic map 2 miles and 79 chains—2.88 miles—east of the Delaware-Maryland border. From the map I determine its geographic coordinates, and enter them as a waypoint in the GPS receiver. The map is stowed away in anticipation of further exploration at a later time.

Not too long thereafter I get a "can you do it yesterday" call for a project in Philadelphia. I plan the details of my trip carefully, finishing my work by noon and scheduling my return trip on a 7:00 p.m. flight. It is a hot and muggy August afternoon. With the map and GPS receiver in hand, my mission is to find the Post Mark'd West. The map indicates that my destination is a point about 800 feet west of Paper Mill Road (County Route 72) just northeast of the Village of Milford Crossroads, Delaware.

I pass the point on Paper Mill Road where the GPS receiver indicates that I am as close as I am going to get to the marker while still on this paved road. The forest to the west of the road is dense, and close to impenetrable. As I drive

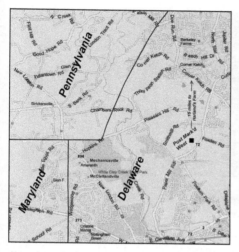

THE POST MARK'D WEST - From Newark drive north on RT 72 (also known as Paper Mill Road). Continue north past Possum Park Road. Watch for an unimproved road on the left. The sign on the arch over it is inscribed WHITE CLAY CREEK STATE PARK. At the point where the road is blocked by a barrier there is a parking lot on the left. A map of the park is mounted under glass on a podium immediately adjacent to the parking lot. The Post Mark'd West is about a fifteen minute walk to the southeast.

farther northeast, the point displayed on the LCD map on the GPS receiver moves farther and farther away. It finally disappears off the edge of the screen, and a sense of disappointment comes over me. So close, but yet so far away.

About half-a-mile further I come upon a sign that reads **WHITE CLAY CREEK STATE PARK.** On it is an arrow that points down a light duty road to the west. My spirits are lifted. Now at least I am headed in the correct direction. About a quarter of a mile down the road I find a parking lot with a sign at the entrance informing visitors of the honor system that is in effect—**FIVE DOLLARS A DAY FOR AN OUT OF STATE VEHICLE.** The rental car has Michigan tags on it, so I reach for my wallet. Before paying, I read the literature posted under glass in an outdoor display case. Among the interesting information about the park is a map showing a trail that meanders along what are mostly corn fields, with a path about a half-mile in that leads off the trail to the south. At the end of the path, marked with an asterisk is the "Mason-Dixon Memorial." I anxiously place a crisp new five dollar bill in the lock box, and attach the GPS receiver to my belt. I also slip my cellular telephone into my shirt pocket and a mini-cassette recorder into my pants pocket, with a bottle of water into the other pocket, and slide the camera case strap over my shoulder. From here on I hoof it down the trail. It's a typical Philadelphia August afternoon—ninety degrees with what feels like equally high humidity. I pause a couple of times along the way and sip from my now-tepid water bottle. The marker that I had read so much about during my decade of research on the Mason Dixon Line is close at hand, and I can feel the adrenaline raising my level of excitement!

The home of the Post Mark'd West – The anchor point of the 233-mile, east-west Mason Dixon Line.

This part of the northwestern state of Delaware is the Piedmont region, an area made up of rolling hills and dense deciduous forests intermingled with farm fields. I am walking through what was once Mr. Alexander Bryan's farm—a place well documented in the journal of the famous surveyors. Two-and-a-third centuries later, it still appears to be producing abundantly. The corn stalks are ten feet high, their pregnant ears bursting with ripe kernels of grain.

It is a slightly sloping downhill walk along the well-mowed trail. About two-tenths of a mile into my hike, I encounter a small wooden footbridge that crosses over what appears to be a nearly-dry drainage ditch. I silently wager to myself that it is what was documented in the June 12th notes in Mason's journal as the "*. . . rivulet of Muddy Run.*" Just past the point where the trail turns east for the third time, the GPS receiver indicates that the object of my search is to the south, several hundred feet into the woods. I turn down the next foot path into the dense forest. There are no markers, and without the aid of the waypoint on the GPS receiver map I would have easily lost my bearings by now. Finally, about 500 feet down the path, I am rewarded by the sight of a cleared area, in the center of which is an old fence. It's horizontal members consist of metal pipes, and it is about three feet high, approximately fifteen feet square, supported by weathered concrete posts at its four corners. In the center stands a three-foot high, four-sided granite marker, twelve inches on a face. On the east side the engraving reads: **POST MARK'D WEST - SET UP BY MASON AND DIXON - JUNE 12, 1764**. On the north: **THIS POST USED AS A BASE IN THE SURVEY OF THE MASON-DIXON LINE 1763-1767**. The side of the marker facing south has no engraving, and the western side is marked with a simple **W**. This marker, of course, is not the original. It was installed in 1953 in the same spot as the original 1764 oak survey post.

I linger for about fifteen minutes, documenting my thoughts on a mini-cassette recorder. The noise of vehicles passing by on Paper Mill Road, muted by the dense foliage, is the only sign that civilization has encroached on what was once an ancient wilderness. I amble around the outside of the fence. The shade of the tall oaks and maples provides a welcome refuge from the searing heat of the August sun. I wonder what sense of adventure and anticipation filled the minds of Charles Mason and Jeremiah Dixon on June 12, 1764—the day they planted their oak anchor post on this exact spot. I ponder the events and the conversations of men that took place at this site many decades ago—at a time before there was even a United States of America—a dozen years before the Declaration of Independence was drawn up and signed.

The granite marker stone, circa 1953,
that stands at the spot where the Mason
Dixon survey crew placed the original oak
POST MARK'D WEST in June 1764.

I step over the rusty pipe that makes up a horizontal member of the protective fence and walk up to the post. I put my hand on the stone that marks the eastern end of one of the most famous survey lines in the Americas. Physical contact with this pillar of history gives me a sense of connection—albeit a distant one—between these men of the 18th century and my 21st century world. Indeed, it could only be a weak connection, as I would never be able to truly appreciate the enormity of the task on which these men were about to embark, and the difficulties they would encounter while doing so. Conversely, even in the wildest of their dreams, they could never envision my 21st century world. How could I begin to explain the marvels of the small electronic device on my belt that almost instantaneously pinpointed my latitude and longitude to within a few feet? Would they take me seriously when I tried to explain the intricacies of the cell phone in my pocket—with no visible connection to the outside world—with which I could communicate in real time with any of the four corners of the earth? How would they react when I told them that in just a few hours I would board an airship that would whisk me home, at the incredible speed of almost 500 miles per hour? It would return me there before the sun would set that very day, to the place near where their adventure would end—233 miles to the west and 3 1/2 years later.

It's difficult for me to pull myself together to leave, for this indeed is a unique place. I reluctantly start my return walk up the path, but I can't help but stop and turn to savor one more glimpse of the stone marker. A sense of emotion inspired by respect for these explorer-surveyors of old comes over me. From this spot they had launched the task that some men of the day deemed impossible to accomplish. I had just been privileged to stand upon the ground where they had once stood—where history was once made.

All the preliminaries had now been put in place. The survey of the great dividing line of latitude between Pennsylvania and Maryland could now commence. The Post Mark'd West would serve as the anchor from which all measurements west along the line would be reckoned. However, there was an unexpected interruption: Mason and Dixon were instructed by the commissioners to drop what they were doing and head to the middle point of the Transpeninsula Line by June 15, 1764. They were to begin the survey and marking of the boundary that divides the present-day states of Delaware and Maryland from this place north. Indeed, the survey notes indicate that the crew departed the day after setting the Post Mark'd West.

The Surveying Of The Tangent Line

⟶THE TRANSPENINSULA LINE⟵

WEDNESDAY - JUNE 13, 1764

"Packing up the Instruments and preparing to set out for the Middle Point (of the Peninsula formed by the Sea and Chesapeake Bay) in order to run the Tangent Line."

The Tangent Line connects two other previously surveyed borders: the Transpeninsula Line to the south and the Twelve Mile Circle (sometimes called the ARC) around New Castle to the north. Before attempting to walk in the footsteps of Mason and Dixon along the Tangent Line, we should first become familiar with these other invisible dividing lines, both of which were previously surveyed and marked by others.

The Delmarva Peninsula is a piece of land that is shared by three states: Delaware, Maryland and Virginia. It is bounded on the east by Delaware Bay and the Atlantic Ocean and the west by Chesapeake Bay. At its southern tip is the fifteen-mile-long Chesapeake Bay Bridge-Tunnel that takes U.S. Route 13 across the mouth of the bay, connecting Cape Charles with Norfolk, Virginia. In times past this land was heavily wooded, but now much of the 180-mile-long peninsula has been cleared. Poultry farms, dairy farms and endless expanses of irrigated corn fields dot the landscape. Agriculture is the dominant industry on this table-top-flat neck of land.

In the mid-18th century, the terrain that now comprises the counties of New Castle, Kent and Sussex was part of Penn's province, and was known as the Lower Three Counties. Two deeds, both dated August 24, 1682, leased this territory for a period of 10,000 years to William Penn. One of those deeds, the deed of *"feoffment"* of Duke of York to William Penn, was for *". . . all that tract of land upon Delaware River and Bay beginning twelve miles from the*

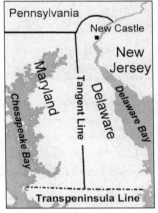

The borders of the lower three counties that now comprise the state of Delaware.

The original marker stone at the eastern end of the Transpeninsula Line sits quietly at the foot of the Fenwick Island Lighthouse.

town of New Castle and extending south to the Horekills, otherwise called "Lopen." Lord Baltimore subsequently, and vigorously, opposed the Penn family's claim.

Human nature hasn't changed much over the intervening 300 years. Throughout history there are accounts of men resorting to violence when they have felt shortchanged by court decisions. Land disputes have led to bloodshed, and history books contain numerous accounts of 17th century farming and fishing villages on the eastern shore of the Lower Three Counties being raided and burned by Marylanders. For example, the entire town of Lewes was burned to the ground in 1673 during such a dispute. In 1685 a royal order divided the territory equally between the Calverts and the Penns. However, contemporary maps were often vague, inaccurate and conflicting, with waterways, settlements and other landmarks mistakenly named on various maps. Such ambiguities in Colonial cartography caused the area of the Lower Three Counties to be about double that intended in the 1682 lease.

Lopen, the southern boundary of the lands referred to in the lease, may be reasonably construed to be what today is Cape Henlopen, located near the town of Lewes. It is situated across Delaware Bay from Cape May, New Jersey. The water between the two capes forms the mouth of Delaware Bay. Lord Baltimore, in 1732, employed John Senex, a cartographer, to prepare a map to be used as evidence in his court battle with the Penns over the location of the borders of their respective provinces. An error showed Cape Henlopen to be located at the site of today's Fenwick Island, more than twenty-five miles south of the Cape Henlopen, on more accurate 21st century maps. This mistake increased the size of Penn's leased lands by about 875 square miles.

The Transpeninsula Line is the line that was surveyed across the Delmarva Peninsula from Fenwick Island, Delaware on the Atlantic Ocean to waters edge on the west side of Taylor's Island on the Chesapeake Bay, more than a decade before Mason and Dixon set foot in the New World. In 1750, Lord Hardwicke, acting head of the Council of Regency, paved the way by decree for the survey and marking of this border. On December 22nd of that year a group of four surveyors—John Emery and Thomas Jones from the Province of Maryland,

and John Watson and William Parsons representing the interests of the Penn family—gathered on the beach of Fenwick Island. Their task was to undertake the task of surveying and marking a line across the peninsula, a line that became known as the Transpeninsula Line. Why they picked the dead of winter to initiate such a task is difficult to understand, unless one considers the absence of pernicious insects and/or leaves on the trees to impede their progress. Before setting off, a spark from their

The Fenwick Island Lighthouse, constructed in the mid-19th century to warn mariners of hidden dangers.

campfire ignited the wood and canvas shelter in which the group had gathered. All hands escaped, but much of their equipment was lost in the conflagration that ensued. A few weeks later, after restocking, the survey got under way again, but progress was once again halted shortly thereafter due to a brutal mid-winter blizzard. Eventually, someone in possession of more practical faculties of mind prevailed! Work on the seventy-mile survey was postponed until early spring. The project was finally completed in mid-June of 1751, with a stone marker having been placed at each mile point.

A white stone that bears the coat of arms of the Calvert family on the south side and that of the Penn Family on the north side marks the eastern terminus of the Transpeninsula Line. It is the original marker, installed in 1751 at the place where the men began their survey. It rests at the curb line on 146th Street, at the foot of the steps leading into the Fenwick Island Lighthouse, about two blocks west of the ocean. The lighthouse—an eighty-five-foot-high aid to navigation—was built in 1858, to warn mariners of the treacherous Fenwick Shoals, at a cost of $23,748. The original light was fueled with whale oil and was visible for fifteen miles out at sea.

⇌ THE 12 MILE CIRCLE AROUND NEW CASTLE ⇌

The original grant for the lands that make up the present State of Delaware states that *"...all lands within 12 miles of the City of New Castle..."*

The New Castle Courthouse - the 12 mile circular northern border of Delaware is centered on the spire of the courthouse.

were to be included. From a practical standpoint, this seemed to be straightforward enough. The circular borderline was surveyed and marked by Isaac Taylor and Thomas Pierson in 1701, under a warrant from William Penn.

However, politics again became involved after-the-fact. What did "*12 miles*" really designate? Marylanders insisted that twelve miles was actually the circumference of the circle, thus allotting the state of Maryland much more territory. Both sides raised the issue of exactly where the center of the circle should be located, and the matter simmered just below the boiling point for many years. In an effort to settle the dispute, commissioners representing the Calverts and the Penns met no less than six times during the 1730s in an effort to resolve their issues, but no resolution was forthcoming.

As a result of ongoing border incidents in the 1730's, everyone involved had come to the breaking point of their patience. The governor of Maryland petitioned the king to render a ruling. Finally, in 1750, Lord Hardwicke handed over a verdict that, among other things, settled the issue of the circle: He reaffirmed that it would be twelve miles in radius, centered on the spire of the dome of the courthouse in New Castle. Did this settle the matter? Apparently not. More controversy arose concerning how the radius should be measured. Marylanders proposed to measure up hills and down valleys. This would give Maryland more land than the strict horizontal measurement technique proposed by the Pennsylvanians. The issue once again went back to an English court to be settled. Eventually the court ruled: The distance would be a twelve mile horizontal measurement. Thus the circular border as marked by the original 1701 survey would stand, and the matter was finally settled.

The old New Castle Courthouse, constructed in 1732, on which the circle was centered, is on Delaware Street in the heart of a several-square-block historic district near the river. When I visit, renovations are in progress, and a sign and yellow construction tape warns off would-be visitors. Small shops, historic buildings and restaurants line the brick sidewalks. Tall trees shade the center square from the impact of the mid-afternoon sun. The humidity on this

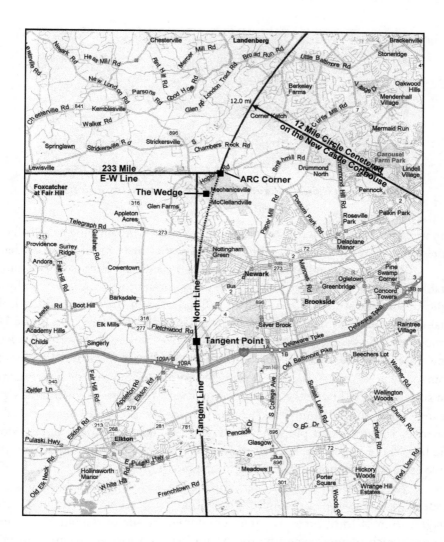

ALL LANDS WITHIN 12 MILES OF THE CITY OF NEW CASTLE - Map detailing the complexity of the borders around the 12 mile New Castle Circle. The circle is centered on the spire of the city hall in the historic district of New Castle. The 82 mile Tangent Line comes in at a slight angle from the midpoint of the Transpeninsula Line. It just touches the circle (tangent to it) near Newark. From this point the border continues directly north—other than allowing for a slight bulge (not visible on this scale map) to accommodate the circle—to the east-west Mason Dixon Line that forms the southern boundary of Pennsylvania. The anchor point for the E-W Line is at the Post Mark'd West – 15 miles south of the Stargazer Stone in Harland's garden – approximately 3 miles inside Delaware.

The Immanuel Episcopal Church (l). Third Street in New Castle (r).

summer day, combined with the suffocating scent of the buttonwood shrubs, is representative of the aroma one might expect to find in an old English garden.

At the north end of the square stands the Immanuel Episcopal Church, established in 1689. A brass plaque on the wall surrounding it and the churchyard indicate that the structure was built in 1703. Stones in the graveyard mark the final resting place of the remains of many generations of believers from the 18th through the 21st century. Some are so weather-beaten that the inscriptions have long since worn off. There is one of a little boy who died in 1777, and another of a woman in her 40s who passed away on February 17, 1788. I run my fingers across the surface of another of the stones. Combining my senses of touch and sight, I barely make out the numbers 1763, the year that Mason and Dixon arrived in America. The notes of a pipe organ waft out through the closed church doors. The bell in the huge steeple clock makes its presence known, announcing with three earth-shaking gongs that it is mid-afternoon.

I return to my car and start the engine, enjoying the advantages of a modern convenience—air conditioning—that generations past could never imagine. Across Third Street is a round building, the site of the old New Castle Library, which is now owned by the New Castle Historical Society. I wonder what stories it would tell if only its walls could talk.

⚞ THE TANGENT LINE ⚟

A new bone of contention between the Penns and Calverts now arose: Was the shore of the Chesapeake located at waters edge of Slaughter's Creek, a strait that separated Taylor's Island from the mainland, about sixty-six miles from the ocean, or was it at western beach of Taylor's Island, sixty-nine miles from the ocean? Not surprisingly, the Calverts favored Slaughter's Creek. This choice would move the mid-point of the line about a mile and a half to the east further than if the later location were chosen. Once again, the issue landed back in court to be settled. In 1760, nine years later, a determination was handed down with the judgment that the line should end at waters edge on the west side of the island. The middle point of the Transpeninsula Line, just under thirty-five miles from the ocean, was then duly marked.

A line is tangent to a circle at the point where it just touches—but does not intersect—its arc. A tangent line will form a right angle with a radius line drawn from the center of the circle or arc. A line running from this mid-point to a point tangent to the twelve mile boundary circle around New Castle would divide the Lower Three Counties from the lands of the Calvert family.

The Tangent Line runs from the mid-point of the Transpeninsula Line to a point tangent to the circle. The survey of the roughly north-south Delaware-Maryland boundary required at least as much skill as the survey and marking of the east-west line that had yet to be initiated. The terrain was certainly more forgiving than the mountains and ravines that Mason and Dixon would later encounter as they moved west, but there were many marshes and swamps with which they would have to contend. The boundary was to run from the mid-point of the Transpeninsula line slightly west of north for almost eighty-two miles. It would proceed across the flat lands of the Delmarva Peninsula through dense woodlands and marshland, across creeks and rivers, and finally finish at a point tangent to the west side of the twelve mile arc-portion of the circle around New Castle. The location of the tangent point would be where this almost eighty-two mile dividing line forms a right angle with a radius line drawn from the belfry of the New Castle Court House to the circular northern border. From this tangent point a line was to run directly north to the east-west line. The effort could best be described as shooting at a target from eighty-two miles away and scoring a direct bull's eye!

A variety of surveyors made earlier attempts in 1751 and 1760 to run this line. In November 1760, John Lukens and Archibald McClain, surveyors from Pennsylvania, and John Priggs and Jonathan Hall, from the Province of Maryland, were appointed by the proprietors of the two colonies to survey the Tangent Line. They devoted three years to the task. The Penns and the Calverts were both obviously impatient with the length of time being spent on this effort, as the August 1763 agreement made with Mason and Dixon for surveying services in the New World included the completion of this assignment as part of their scope of effort.

Today, the north-south Tangent Line is also recognized as the Mason Dixon Line. However, the noted Englishmen's attachment to this boundary is not quite as celebrated as to that of their longer 233-mile east-west line.

SATURDAY - JUNE 23, 1764

"Engaged ax men, etc. amounting to 39 The whole company including Steward, tent keepers, Cooks, Chain carriers, etc. amounting to 39. Two Wagons, Eight Horses, etc."

⊷ THE GREAT POCOMOKE SWAMP ⊷

THURSDAY - SEPTEMBER 13, 1764

". . . went to see Pokomoke Swamp; It's about 30 Miles in Length and 14 in breadth; (The West Line from the sea passes through it.): There is the greatest quantity of Timber I have ever saw: Above the tallest Oak, Beech, Poplar, Hickory, Holly and Fir; Towers the lofty Cedar: (without a Branch), till its ever green conical top; seems to reach the clouds: The pleasing sight of which; renewed my wishes to see Mount Lebanon."

Jumping forward in the survey journal by several months, I schedule a trip to the great swamp, when I travel from Fenwick Island to the mid-point on the Transpeninsula Line. Mason usually took his side trips on Sunday, his day of rest. This week in September, however, was different. The survey notes indicate that on the preceding Sunday he was involved with replacing the temporary wood markers with permanent stone markers at the ten, fifteen and twenty mile points along the Tangent Line. On this occasion we catch him slipping away from the group on a Thursday to visit Pocomoke Swamp—shown on modern maps as the Great Cypress Swamp.

The fifty-square-mile freshwater swamp—somewhat smaller than Mason's estimate—straddles the Transpeninsula Line. Most of it is located in Delaware, with a smaller part in Maryland. The notes of John Watson, one of the surveyors of the Transpeninsula Line, detail the difficulty the group had making their way through the shoulder-high water, quicksand and poison ivy vines that were found in this vast expanse of snake-infested, water-saturated spongy land. It is home to the northernmost stand of Bald Cyprus [*Taxodium distichum*] trees in the United States. Mason described the canopy of trees in the swamp in some places as being more than one hundred feet high. The Great Cypress Swamp provides shelter to more than seventy species of birds, raccoons, and flying squirrels. Several species of snakes and frogs also inhabit this marshland.

Corn and wheat fields are now planted in what was once the wilderness of the Great Pocomoke Swamp (l). A tiny glimpse of yesteryear – what the appearance of the swamp may have been two-and-a-half centuries ago (r).

The major industry in the towns and villages on the periphery of the swamp for many years was the production of hand-hewn cypress shingles. Cypress wood possesses the quality of resisting rot when exposed to moisture.

I was somewhat disappointed when I visited the swamp on a Thursday morning, 240 years after Mason's stopover. The area is no longer as wild and untamed as he found it in 1764. Progress has intervened. Much of the swamp has been drained, and the timber has been cut. so only a minor glimpse into times past still exists. An occasional isolated dense stand of oak, beech, poplar, hickory and holly can still be found, located between oceans of irrigated corn fields. The stagnant waters of the swamp have given way to arrow-straight, man-made drainage channels. None of the lofty cedars Mason described in his journal are to be found today.

The road bridges a waterway as it winds through one of the few remaining dense stands of trees. Just past the bridge, I bring the car to a halt. I get out and walk back to the bridge, which spans a drainage channel. The sight line down the creek is visible for about 100 yards or so. The overhanging foliage and vines duplicate the appearance of a tropical jungle, with the odor of decaying organic material hanging heavy in the misty morning air. Everything seems to be in shadow, as the mid-morning sun illuminates only tiny patches of earth and water. The near 100 percent humidity reinforces my perception of what it might be like to experience the isolation of standing on the edge of a waterway deep in the Amazon jungle. Birds chirp and squawk, alerting their kin to the presence of a stranger in their midst. High above me branches shutter as a squirrel leaps from tree to tree. As I glance around, my eyes fall on the largest bullfrog I have ever seen, sitting motionless in one of the sunlit spots no more than ten feet away. He startles me

The mid-point of the Transpeninsula Line. The southwest corner of Delaware.

as much as my sudden appearance does the same to him, and we both stare at one other. Obviously, he is hoping that I am unaware of his presence. Having no interest in molesting the amphibian, I take a slow step back, intending to get into my car, and his spring-like legs instantly propel him five feet in a single leap off the muddy bank and into the murky water.

⇥ RENDEZVOUS AT THE MIDDLE POINT ⇤

MONDAY - JUNE 25, 1764
"Crossed the River Nanticoke in canoes and went to the Middle Point, Fixed up the transit Instrument and began to produce an arch of a Great Circle in the direction of the last run."

The corps of thirty-nine men, led by Charles and Jeremiah, arrived at the middle point on June 25th. They quickly located the previously-set middle point marker. Wasting no time, the group immediately began the trek back to the north, and by the end of the next day they had set the third milepost.

I am moving west on Route 54 at the speed limit when, without warning, the southwest corner of Delaware suddenly comes up on me. It is to the right—on the north side of the road—as I travel west. There is a huge truck in my rear view mirror bouncing down the highway about twenty feet behind me, and its bumper appears to be precariously close—at the level of my rear window! I dare not hit the brakes to make an abrupt stop, so I speed up a bit to put some distance between us. About a quarter-mile further down the road, I see a road veering off to the left. I gradually slow down, put on my signal and make the turn off of Route 54. The driver of the monster truck leans on his air horn to vent his displeasure with me. I turn the car around in a driveway and retrace my tracks.

On the north side of the road there is a cutoff with room for parking. As soon as I pull in, another car pulls in behind me. A young man gets out and engages me in conversation. A would-be cartographer, he is in the process of giving thought to pursuing a mapmaking career. Although he lives within a few miles distance, he has never before been to the stone, and it is only by sheer happenstance that we encounter each other on this day. The map on the GPS receiver fascinates him. A marvel of modern day technology, its cursor pinpoints our location at the southwest corner of Delaware.

A Mason Dixon Crownstone marks the mid-point of the Transpeninsula Line. A bricked walkway leads up to its enclosure. An attempt at landscaping on either side of the footpath that is intended to add elegance to the spot has fallen prey to the ravages of time and thoughtless people. The dead flowers and

A peek inside the doorless cage that houses the original Crownstone and three other unidentified markers.

trampled down plants give the impression that no one cares. The Crownstone and three other unmarked stones are protected from vandals and the weather by what can best be described as an animal cage with a roof. One of the other monuments is no doubt from the earlier survey, which marked the mid-point of the line. The cage keeps people out, rather than the markers in! The irresistible urge to toss coins into a pond of water has carried over to the caged stones. Many pennies, nickels and dimes lay on the ground inside the cage. A few have hit their intended mark and rest on the flat surface top of the Crownstone.

Not wishing to reinvent the wheel, Mason and Dixon followed the general *"...direction of the last run"* that was set out by their predecessors in earlier efforts just a few years previous. The last run, however, did not produce an acceptably straight line. Mason was determined to do better. As long as the line was straight, he could calculate a table of offsets for each milepost. New markers were set at each mile. As meticulously documented in their journal, advancement to the north across the flat lands of the Delmarva Peninsula was fairly rapid, with three mileposts being set on some days.

⇒ SHARPTOWN ⇐

FRIDAY - JUNE 29, 1764
"Fixed the 6th Mile Post"

Just to the west of this post is the village of Sharptown, named after the Honorable Horatio Sharpe, Royal Governor of the Province of Maryland

The carnival at Sharptown (l). The dead end of Ferry Street (r).

when Mason and Dixon passed by in the 18th century. Mason made numerous references to His Excellency in his notes, taking great pains to keep Sharpe and other dignitaries of note in both provinces abreast of the progress being made on the task for which he was commissioned.

The lands surrounding this town were once rife with timber. The wide breadth of the Nanticoke River on the north edge of town provided a water route to the Chesapeake Bay. The site was a natural for becoming a center for shipbuilding in Colonial America. A man with the auspicious name of Matthew Marine settled in this spot along the river in 1818. He immediately took advantage of the location and the abundance of raw material that surrounded him, and founded the Sharptown Marine Railway Company. By the end of the 19th century, Matthew's company had constructed eighteen merchant vessels registered in the United States.

Today Sharptown is a quiet village with little visible industry. Shipbuilding came to an end in 1919, when the boat company went bankrupt, and a large box manufacturing plant burned to the ground in the early 1950s. I begin my tour at the south end of town. From a distance I spy a Ferris wheel, a sure sign of a visiting carnival. However, as I come closer I discover what appears to be an abandoned amusement park, with rides and cotton candy stands. Not a soul is in sight, and being a curious fellow, I have to take a closer look. I get out of the car and begin to stroll among the rides. They all sit motionless, as if suspended in time, starring back at this stranger who dares to walk among them. I imagine that I hear the sounds of a calliope, and if I close my eyes I can see a thousand laughing children running around in a hundred different directions devouring the delights of the carnival.

Suddenly, out of the blue, a voice rings out, "Can I help you?"

I am startled, almost at a loss for words. There stands an elderly bearded man no more than six feet in front of me. My gut reaction is to blurt out "Where did you come from?" It takes a fraction of a second for me to gain my composure. I sputter "Err…yes…can you tell me anything about this abandoned carnival?"

"What makes you think this is abandoned, son? You must be a visitor to town, as everyone here knows that this is a permanent fixture. Been here for more years that most can remember. The lights come on, the music starts and the rides all come to life, regular as clockwork, every year, in the month of August."

The Sharptown Volunteer Fire Company owns the carnival. It becomes the center of attraction for several weeks in this town of 650 people, the highlight of its summer season. For the other forty-eight weeks of the year it sits silently, just waiting to take its place in the limelight come the 1st of August.

On this late June day the village gives me the impression of a ghost town. It is high noon, with nary a moving car in sight. Aside from the bearded man, I can only see a young woman pushing a baby carriage along one of the side streets. What remains of the approach to an old drawbridge is barricaded at the end of Ferry Street. I walk past the graffiti-marred barricade, and note a pleasure boat making its way down river. Several folks wave to me, and I reciprocate. A large bird swoops down and plucks a lunch of raw seafood from the water. Prior to the erection of the drawbridge, a ferry transported horses, wagons and people from one side of the river to the other. In even earlier times, canoes owned by the Nanticoke Indians transported Charles and Jeremiah across the river and back again. Today, a soft drink machine with its door falling off its hinges stands sentinel to an era that has come to a close. To the east is a high level bridge, with enough clearance for medium-sized craft. It now carries Route 313 across the river on its way out of town.

⤚ THE RIVER NANTICOKE ⤙
HOME OF THE TIDEWATER PEOPLE

SATURDAY - JUNE 30, 1764
"Produced the Line across the River Nanticoke. Measured the breadth of the River by angles taken by a Hadley's Quadrant and a Base Line upon the North Side of the River. Entrance of the River from the Middle Point is 6 Miles 70 Chains 25 Links."

In the early summer of 1608 Captain John Smith set out from Jamestown to explore the numerous tributaries of Chesapeake Bay. He ventured into Tangier

The Nanticoke River at Sharptown.

Sound, and came upon the fifty-mile-long waterway that today is known as the Nanticoke River, which is navigable from the bay to Seaford, Delaware. Smith named it for the Nanticoke Indians who inhabited its shores. Nanticoke translated means "tidewater people" or "those who ply the tidal stream."

In his notes of June 25th, Mason indicated that the party crossed the Nanticoke in canoes on their way south to the mid-point. It seems logical that he had bartered with "those who ply the tidal stream" for passage across the river. Knowing that he had much foresight, he probably bargained for a round trip, as he and his crew were back in the area in need of crossing again just two weeks later.

The woodlands along the Nanticoke play host to a wide variety of deciduous and evergreen trees. Red maple, along with several species of pine and oak, thrive in the river's watershed. In turn the thick growth of trees and underbrush supplies food and shelter to bald eagles, peregrine falcons, otter, beaver and white-tailed deer. The river itself teems with perch, pickerel, trout, catfish, rockfish and large mouth bass. Blue crabs are abundant in the lower Nanticoke, and this shell fish supports one of the most viable commercial fishing industries in the area.

The river has remained largely unchanged with the passage of time. It provides the observer with a momentary glimpse of what Mason and Dixon and their entourage must have experienced as they chained their way north across it on a Saturday in 1764.

⟶ THE HAUNTED VILLAGE OF RELIANCE ⟵

THURSDAY - JULY 5, 1764
"Put down the 12th, 13th and 14th Mile Posts"

Traveling on Route 531, I am now entering the village of Reliance from the south. The street signs appropriately call it Line Road, as the road straddles the state dividing line. Those who live on the east side are residents of Delaware, while their neighbors across the street are Marylanders. The USGS map shows the 12th milepost of the Tangent Line standing at the end of Line Road, right smack in the middle of town. I look, but can't locate it. Delaware Route 20 becomes Maryland Route 392 as it crosses the border. Maryland Route 577 and Woodland Road also converge at a slight offset at this point. It's a place truly befitting its original name—Johnson's Corners—for indeed it is a crossroads with many corners.

Welcome to Reliance: the 19th century home of Patty Cannon.

While I search for Mason and Dixon's stone marker, I am sidetracked by another historical marker at the corner of Route 577 that points out Patty Cannon's house. The dwelling is no more than a few hundred feet west of the dividing line. Across the street, just inside Delaware, is a cemetery. Some of the stone markers identify the final resting place of folks who lived in the 1800s. If only they could talk they would have some bone-chilling stories to tell.

During the 18th century and into the first half of the 19th century the Delmarva Peninsula was the main transportation route for the Underground Railroad. Names can be deceiving: The railroad was a system through which slaves from the south escaped to freedom in the north. It was neither literally underground in a tunnel nor was it a road for a train with wooden ties, steel spikes and iron rails. Railway terms were used to disguise the activities of the system's secret. Various escape routes were called *lines*, and stopping off places or safe houses were *stations*. Those who aided the operation of the system, including religious groups and abolitionists, were referred to as *conductors*, and the escaping slaves were known as *packages* or *freight*. It is estimated that more than 40,000 black men, women and children traveled the railway, after being hidden in stations and abetted by conductors, during the later 1700s and the first sixty years of the 1800s.

In Colonial times this main line through the peninsula was a treacherous corridor through which to navigate. Prudence kept runaways off the trails and primitive roads in the area, lest they be spotted and captured. While the numerous swamps, marshes, creeks and heavily wooded forests provided excellent camouflage from slave catchers, they also presented enormous dangers to the escapees. The area was dotted with quicksand pits; in addition, one had to constantly watch out

The haunted house of Patty Cannon at Johnson's Crossroads, where the noted kidnapping group had headquarters, as described in George Alfred Townsend's novel "The Entailed Hat." The house borders on Caroline and Dorchester Counties and the state of Delaware.

for poisonous snakes and wild animals. Death from hunger and drowning was also a possibility, and in the summer the marshes supported clouds of disease-carrying mosquitoes. Yet, the burning desire for freedom inspired this horde of humanity to brave these difficulties and dangers while traveling the railway north.

A village, town or city, can't, on its own, become notorious. It is only by the cruel and evil acts of infamous people that the place can become widely and unfavorably known. Lucretia Hanley Cannon came to the untamed frontier of the Delmarva Peninsula from Canada at the dawn of the 19th century. Patty, as she was known, was a large, muscular, boisterous woman who was a match for any man. She married Joe Johnson, and they lived near the intersection of what is now Routes 577 and 392 in Reliance, Maryland. The pair ran a tavern, across the street in Delaware, where Patty could be frequently found tending bar. In addition to serving corn whiskey from one side of the bar, she also served as bouncer on the other side. She often demonstrated her great strength by wrestling unruly patrons to the floor, and physically threw them out into the street afterwards. However, it wasn't her great strength, her bar tending abilities, or her wrestling skills that live on today as the Legend of Patty Cannon.

As a sideline to being innkeepers, she and her husband ran what can best be described as a reverse Underground Railroad. In plain-talk they ran a kidnapping ring. They, and their associates, abducted runaway slaves and free blacks, took them south and sold them into slavery to plantation owners in Georgia. Local stories that have been handed down through generations tell of their captives being brought to their home in shackles. They were then chained to the walls of the attic in the oppressive summer heat, or cast into the shivering winter dampness of the basement. When the house was overfilled with captives, the trees in the surrounding forest served as restraining posts. Here individuals would languish for days or weeks, with little access to food or water. The close confinement of many people made for putrid conditions. When the dungeons filled up and the supply of available trees dwindled, the crowd of human cargo was herded into horse drawn covered wagons and transported to Woodland Ferry on the Nanticoke River, a few miles to the southeast of Reliance. From there they were crowded into the hold of a wooden sailing vessel and transported down river, through Chesapeake Bay to a port in Georgia.

While slavery was legal in both Maryland and Delaware during the first half of the 19th century, some of Patty's activities ran afoul of the law. The locals were afraid of her and her cronies, and were unwilling to report them to the authorities or, heaven forbid, appear in a court of law and testify against them. On the rare occasion when the sheriff did arrive from one jurisdiction, Patty would conveniently be untouchable, just across the street in the other state. This went on for many years.

Eventually, in 1822, after some coordination, lawmen from both Delaware and Maryland simultaneously raided Reliance. Patty was arrested by the authorities from Delaware and charged with, among other crimes, ten murders, to which she confessed. She was hauled off to a prison in Georgetown. End of story? Not quite. Patty had the last laugh. While being interrogated by the jailer, Patty popped a cyanide capsule into her mouth right before his eyes. The poison claimed her before the gallows could.

It was lunch time. I looked for Patty's tavern on the east side of the dividing line in Delaware before I left town. Perhaps I'd have a cold drink and a sandwich on this hot and humid afternoon. It was nowhere to be found.

⊷ WOODLAND FERRY ⊶

The village of Woodland is about four miles southeast of Reliance. The five-minute drive from Reliance transports one back through several centuries of time. The banks of the Nanticoke River abound in vegetation, including lily pads that look big enough and substantial enough to walk on. The sound of birds chirping as they come and go through the heavily wooded forests on both sides of the river make one want to sit back and just let time pass by. The setting hasn't changed much in the more than two centuries that have transpired since Mason and Dixon passed just to the west. Woodland Ferry—formerly known as Cannon's Ferry (no relation to Patty)—the embarkation point of the infamous 19th century slave ship—was in operation before Mason and Dixon's visit to the area. Although no firm date has been established, the first ferry crossing at this point could have been as early as 1671. Officially, the state of Delaware issued a permit for operation of the ferry on February 2, 1793. It was owned and operated

The Virginia C, *a cable ferry, plies the waters of the Nanticoke between Woodland Ferry and Bethel, Delaware.*

by Isaac and Betty Cannon, and then later by their sons. The ferry carried horses, carriages, wagons and passengers across the Nanticoke from Woodland to Bethel. It was powered by the ferrymen, horses, ropes and notched poles. Customers were sometimes pressed into service to move the ferry across the 500-foot-wide river.

In 1843 the Delaware Legislature empowered Sussex County to take over the service. The legislation required that "all citizens of the State, with their wagons and carriages, should be transported across the ferry at all times between sunrise and sunset free of charge." Today the state of Delaware operates the cable-run ferry. The horses, ropes and notched poles are gone, but the ferry ride is still free. The sixty-five-foot-long steel, diesel powered, cable-drawn *Virginia C* can transport three or four cars across the river in just under three minutes.

The captain seemed almost embarrassed when I asked him if the stories about the slave ship embarking from this place were true. "Yes, and there's even more to the story," he said. "Slaves were frequently pressed into service to power the ferry. Many drowned at this very spot when they collapsed and fell into the river due to exhaustion."

Before driving onto the ferry for my free ride across the water I pause, sitting for a few moments to admire the place. The fragrance of flowers fills the air, and I silently watch as a bee checks each flower painstakingly before moving on the next. The sight of birds fluttering freely into and out of the forest gives this river edge a sense of serenity and peacefulness. It's hard to imagine that such atrocities could have taken place in the past on this tranquil spot on the River Nanticoke. Free—almost free—and then captured, shackled and returned to a life of slavery. The tears that were shed here in this place probably could have filled this river. The screams of anguish that must have echoed through the forest as the human beings were cruelly tossed into the hold of the wooden slave ship two centuries ago surely would have drowned out the delightful babble of a thousand birds that fill the air on this June afternoon.

⇻ SEAFORD: THE NYLON CAPITAL OF THE WORLD ⇼

The 18th Century plantation mansion of Henry Harrison Ross.

The family name of Dupont is well recognized in the state of Delaware. In 1939 the Dupont Company built its first nylon manufacturing plant in this town on Route 13 in southern Delaware. The industry has been the catalyst for a great deal of economic development in this part of the Delmarva Peninsula. Its corporate headquarters have been in Wilmington for almost as long as anyone can remember.

Seaford is located just a few miles to the east of Woodland Ferry, at the head of the Nanticoke River. The first known inhabitants of the area were the Nanticoke Indians, who settled here in about 4000 BCE. The first record of European settlement in what is now Seaford was that of Jeremiah Jadwin, who was granted a 1750 acre plot of land along the river in 1672. His presence here preceded Mason and Dixon's survey by almost a century.

As in much of Colonial America, agriculture was the primary enterprise in early Seaford. Tobacco was the dominant revenue-producing crop, and in some locales it was actually used as currency. It would not have been uncommon to make an arrangement to compensate a worker with a certain measure of tobacco in return for labor that he performed.

William Henry Harrison Ross was a large landowner in this part of Delaware. His main interests were farming and politics. At the age of thirty-six he was the youngest man ever to be elected governor. He served his one four-year elected term in office that is permitted by the Delaware Constitution from 1851 to 1855. In 1859 he constructed a mansion on his 1395-acre agricultural estate. The structure has been restored to its 19th century elegance. The quarters for the slaves that worked the Ross plantation have also been renovated. Both stand as testimony to an age and era that is long past.

Lurking in the shadows of the trees, watching over Mud Mill Pond, is Mile Post 42 (l). The mirror surface of Mud Mill Pond where the Tangent Line crosses it near Mile Post 42 (r).

⸬ CHOPTANK MILLS: MILE POST 42 ⸬

THURSDAY - JUNE 26, 1764
"Produced the line and set the 42nd and 43rd Mile Posts"

Choptank Mills is just a dot on the USGS map, but its name and location on the map adjacent to Mud Mill pond intrigued me. I was hoping to find an old, abandoned picturesque mill in this place, but in the back of my mind I was sure that the mill would be a thing of the past. I had done some research beforehand and found that the millstone from the historic gristmill that had once stood on this spot was now on display in the Delaware Agricultural Museum in Dover. The dot on the map takes its name from the Choptank River that meanders through the area, a waterway that in turn borrows its name from the tribe of Native Americans that once inhabited the area.

As I approach the area on Mud Mill Road I see a sign—**CHOPTANK MILLS**—with an arrow pointing to the right. I get my hopes up. Maybe, just maybe, there really would be an old, rustic mill. However, it was not to be. There are several majestic log homes, but no mill.

About a quarter mile down the road, I encounter Mud Mill Pond. A dam just off the north shoulder of the road holds back the waters of this tributary of the Choptank River. It seems as if time has passed this place by. The scene of the pond with an angler in a rowboat a hundred feet or so offshore is one that would make a perfect subject for a calendar.

Another quarter-mile west further down the road is a Y-junction, where Mud Mill and Wolf Road converge. In the crotch of the Y, about a hundred feet from the edge of the waters of the pond, in the shadows of a group of tall trees, is Mile Post 42. Fish break the surface, hoping for a breakfast of insects that venture too low over the water. I long for a fishing pole. What a way to spend a June morning—lost in the wilderness along the Mason Dixon Line drowning worms in hopes that the big one will bite.

⚓ MARYDEL: A TOWN DIVIDED ⚓

MONDAY - JULY 30, 1764
". . . fixed the 45th and 46th"

Mile marker 45, a Crownstone, brandishing the coats of arms of the two Colonial families, stands in the middle of the present-day town of Marydel— or perhaps better stated, marks the dividing line between the two towns of Marydel—one in Delaware and the other in Maryland.

In 1850, William Hall purchased a huge tract of forested land that spilled across the dividing line. Halltown, named for its founder, soon boasted a sawmill and three houses. In 1853 the village was renamed Marydel, in recognition of the two states in which it was located. The town grew quickly, and within the next few years two hotels, a fruit evaporating factory, a school and a church were established. Soon the railroad—a real railroad consisting of iron rails, wooden ties and noisy smoke belching steam locomotives—arrived in Marydel. This branch of the Philadelphia, Baltimore & Washington Railroad (P. B. & W.) began at Clayton, Delaware and eventually extended to Oxford, Maryland and on to the Chesapeake Bay.

I begin my visit by looking for signs of the railroad that once ran through town, but there is certainly no railroad here. The USGS map shows tracks that cross the diiding line and run diagonally through the two villages. Perhaps I am looking in the wrong place. The evidence of a time when trains traversed the two Marydels is elusive. The only testimony to an iron horse ever having visited Marydel are the barely-exposed tops of steel rails that peek through the asphalt paving on Strauss Street. To the north of the street, they disappear into a heavily wooded area, where mature trees have grown up between the ties. To the south, relics of the old tracks run between the tree line and a vacant lot. More than likely, this was the scene of the once-busy Marydel train station.

The town is quiet, with little activity. I notice a young man washing a fire engine on the tarmac in front of the Marydel Volunteer Fire Company

A relic of the past: the remnants of the railroad tracks as they cross Strauss Street in Marydel. According to the USGS Map, the old Marydel Railroad Station once stood just ahead and to the left.

and a farmer on his tractor crossing the dividing line from east to west. The driver of a pickup truck sounds a beep on his horn to warn me of his approach as I kneel down to take a picture of the iron rails as they pass into the grass at roadside.

On a damp, dreary December morning in 1876, back when trains were the kings of land transportation, a steam locomotive pulling several passenger cars and a mail car pulled into Marydel. The whistle stop for the train was brief. Several mail bags were thrown off through the open door of the mail car onto the platform, and the station master tossed a couple back to the man in the open doorway. The mighty steam engine and its cars stretched from one end of the small town to the other, blocking Strauss Street to the north and the trail that now is Route 20 to the south. About two dozen passengers embarked, while several others got on the train. Among the new arrivals in town were two impeccably dressed strangers. Three attendants accompanied each man. In a matter of minutes the mighty locomotive's steam-driven whistle thundered out a warning that the train was about to depart from the station, spewing out a huge plume of smoke and steam, and issuing an earthshaking grunt as it chugged out of town. The group of eight—minus one—hiked south along the tracks. If you stretch the limits of your imagination today, you can envision the remnants of the old right-of-way to the south, through an area where the trees seem to be a little less mature than those that surround them. The men disappeared into a clearing in the forest. The lone man that stayed behind had a briefcase stuffed with cash. He hurriedly made arrangements with a farmer for the use of two horse drawn carriages. Obviously, he was planning a fast getaway.

Suddenly, two gunshots emanated from the woodlands. A few minutes later, the pair of dapperly-dressed gentlemen and their entourage appeared back in town. Four of them stepped into one of the carriages and quickly departed on the road toward Dover. The other three, joined by the purchasing agent, piled into the other coach. They cracked the whip over the horses and exited town on the road toward Clayton.

For many years rumors floated around the two Marydels as to what had transpired on that gloomy December morning. Eventually, years later, a man on his deathbed revealed the well kept secret. He had been part of the group of eight. The two well-dressed gentlemen were James Bennett, a famous journalist from New York and Paris, and Fred May, a noted world explorer from Baltimore. The two had had a falling out over a woman. They had a dispute to settle, but since dueling was illegal in almost every province of the New World, Marydel seemed like an out-of-the-way place to put an end to it. Pistols were the weapons of choice, and each was loaded with one bullet. As was the customary format for a duel, the pair stood back-to-back and then walked off a pre-agreed number of paces. They then quickly turned toward one another. May fired and narrowly missed his opponent, and Bennett slowly and deliberately raised his firearm and pointed it directly at May's chest. He paused for a second, and then raised the weapon up higher before pulling the trigger. It discharged harmlessly into the air, and the two antagonists quickly left Marydel before the authorities could be summoned to arrest them for their illegal activity.

⚬ THE DELAWARE AND CHESAPEAKE CANAL ⚬

As early as the mid-1600s Augustine Herman, a Dutch envoy and cartographer, recognized that the Delaware River and the Chesapeake Bay were separated by a narrow strip of land, about fifteen miles in width, at the neck of the Delmarva Peninsula. He suggested that it might be practical to build a waterway connecting the two. This would eliminate about 300 miles of the water route between Baltimore and Philadelphia.

MONDAY - AUGUST 20, 1764
"Set the 74th Mile Post"

TUESDAY - AUGUST 21, 1764
"Ditto. 75th and 76th. Crossed Broad Creek"

Back Creek, Peach Creek and Long Creek are shown in the area of the 74th, 75th and 76th mileposts of the Tangent Line on the Elkton USGS typographic 7.5 minute map. Broad Creek seems to be conspicuous by its absence. Perhaps the Broad Creek of 1764, as mentioned in the survey journal, was one of the small meandering creeks and streams that crisscrossed the peninsula before man intervened and converted it into Herman's vision of a waterway for oceangoing ships and barges—the Delaware and Chesapeake Canal. The canal's

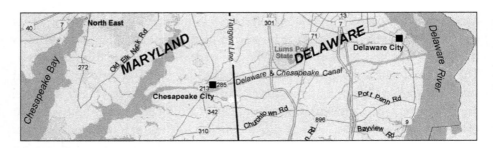

The Delaware & Chesapeake Canal as it makes its way for fifteen miles across the neck of the Delmarva Peninsula from Chesapeake City, Maryland to Delaware City, Delaware.

eastern terminus is at Reedy Point in Delaware City, Delaware, and it eventually empties into Back Creek, a tributary of the Chesapeake Bay, at Chesapeake City, Maryland. The Tangent Line crosses it just east of Chesapeake City.

After a first attempt to dig a canal was abandoned in the early 1800s, the canal was built along its present route, financed by private enterprise, at a cost of 2.5 million dollars. The waterway opened for business in October 1829. The canal had four locks on two levels, and could accommodate sailing ships and barges with a maximum draft of ten feet. About thirteen miles of it consisted of a lock where the water level was about sixteen feet above sea level. In the 18th century, teams of horses and mules towed vessels along the canal and through its locks.

The United States government purchased the canal from its private owners in 1919. The four locks were eliminated, and the depth of the waterway was increased to twenty-seven feet at low tide. In addition, the width of the facility was expanded to 400 feet. The waterway became capable of carrying ship traffic in both directions.

In the mid-1970s, the U.S. Army Corps of Engineers made further improvements. Today, forty percent of the maritime ship traffic that leaves or arrives at the Port of Baltimore travels this 450-foot-wide, 35-foot-deep sea level navigation channel that runs across the upper neck of the Delmarva Peninsula. As part of the Intercoastal Waterway, it is one of the busiest man-made waterways in the world, and one of only two major sea level shipping canals being used in America in the 21st Century.

The banks of the canal provide several good sites for those who enjoy prospecting for fossils. Shells, along with reptile and fish bones, vertebrae and teeth, are abundant in the dredge spoils near St. Georges and at the foundation of the Reedy Point Bridge. The small-scale collecting of fossils for private collections is permitted, but Federal law prohibits the collection of fossils from these areas for commercial purposes.

Mile Post 74 on the Tangent Line sits several hundred feet south of the canal at the rear of Bethel Cemetery. It is on a hill elevated thirty feet or so above the water's surface. During my visit there has been recent rain, and there are puddles of water everywhere. The odor of decaying grass cuttings hang heavy in the hot and humid air. Tiger lilies have pushed their way through the perimeter fence

Looking east on the canal where the Tangent Line crosses it.

just adjacent to the marker. Oddly, the plants are rooted in Delaware but blooming in Maryland. Wild raspberries, not yet quite ripe, are growing in the underbrush adjacent to the mowed grass. At the entrance to the cemetery sits a 30-foot-high concrete cross with a plaque at its base which tells the story of the Bethel Methodist Church and Cemetery.

The Chesapeake and Delaware Canal Museum is just a quarter mile to the west of Bethel Cemetery. It is well worth the half-hour that it takes to walk through the exhibits. The pictures and the displays tell the entire story from the original 14-mile-long, 10-feet-deep, 36-foot-wide locked canal that opened in 1829 to the modern, present-day waterway.

The museum is located in the original canal pump house. On display in their original positions are the cypress waterwheel lift pump and the two 175-horse-power steam engines that turned it. A channel was dug from Back Creek to the pump house. It emptied into a 22-foot-deep well. The wheel turned at only one-and-a-half revolutions per minute but could lift 1,200,000 gallons of water per hour into the lock. The pump wheel was in continuous service for seventy-six years and suffered only one breakdown during that entire period.

The museum is air-conditioned. The controlled temperature and humidity is a welcome respite from the summer heat. The two gigantic steam engines are painted a shiny black, and the rooms in which they sit are spotlessly clean. I was the only one there in the pump room that day, and the silence is a bit unnerving. I wonder what it must have been like to be there on a June afternoon 150 years ago. If it was hot outside on that day, it must have been sweltering in the room that housed the steam engines. Silence in such a place would have been unknown—the roar of the machinery along with the racket created by the

The Bethel Cross marks the location of the original Bethel Methodist Church that was built on the site in 1780 (l). The building was demolished in 1965 to make way for the widening of the canal. A stone among stones—the oldest marker in the cemetery, placed at this spot by Mason & Dixon in 1764. At the back of the Bethel Cemetery Mile Post 74 quietly watches over hundreds of 19th and 20th century tombstones.

gigantic wheel as it lifted more than 13,000 gallons of water a minute would have been enough to awaken the dead.

Today's sea level canal is capable of handling all but the largest of oceangoing ships. It eliminates the 300-mile trip from Baltimore, down the Chesapeake Bay, around Cape Charles and then back up the coast on the route to Europe. Forty percent of the ship traffic that comes and goes through the Port of Baltimore uses this waterway, and the canal handles more than 15,000 commercial and pleasure vessels each year, making it one of the busiest canals in the world.

⁕ CHESAPEAKE CITY ⁕

Chesapeake City, population 735, is just to the west of the Tangent Line where it crosses the canal. The 232 acres of dry land that it resides on are split in half by the canal. The north and south sides of town are joined by Route 213, which passes over the waterway on an arch suspension bridge, which offers clearance to all but the largest of ships. The massive structure in the center of town overshadows the city from every vantage point. I turn around in a vacant lot, and stop under one of its gigantic supporting piers, feeling like an ant in the shadow of an elephant. The original vertical lift drawbridge, at this location, was destroyed when an oil tanker—the *Franz Klasen*—struck it in 1942.

Chesapeake City was originally known as Bohemia Village. In 1829 it sported only two structures: Chick's Tavern and a lock house for collecting tolls on the canal. The streets are narrow; the buildings are quaint; the atmosphere is nautical. The downtown area of Chesapeake City is on the National Historic Registry. Restaurants, bed and breakfasts and souvenir shops abound.

It was lunch time. I pull into the Tap Room Bar & Restaurant on the south side of town. Even before entering I suspected that the place was appropriately named. A large truck was blocking one lane of the narrow street in front of the establishment. The driver was unloading keg after keg after keg, dragging them into the basement of the tavern on an oversized hand truck. Once I was inside, my suspicions are confirmed. There is

The RT 213 bridge dominates the skyline of Chesapeake City.

an abundance of spigots available for the dispensing of the liquid made from malt and fermented hops, commonly known as beer.

A couple sits at a nearby table. On it are stacked a pile of discarded crab shells, a plentiful supply of steamed crabs and a large pitcher of cold beer. They pay little attention to my gaze, as they are occupied cracking open crabs and carefully extracting every last morsel of the tasty white meat. On the wall behind them is a sign: **JUMBO STEAMED CRABS - $44.00 PER DOZEN**. At that price you can't afford to waste even one small tidbit.

I would have loved to have joined them. During my childhood and young adult days in New Jersey, so near to the seashore, eating crabs was a ritual. We would all go crabbing in hopes of bringing home a bushel or two of the ugly looking bay-dwellers. Gathered around a large pot of boiling water that had been spiked with Mom's secret blend of spices, we tossed the crabs in one-by-one, making every effort to avoid their pinchers. One of the critters would invariably get dropped onto the kitchen floor. With a growl and a snarl of "how dare you invade my turf," Ollie, our miniature dachshund, would scamper after it, frequently getting nipped on the nose in the process. We would then strip the dining room table and cover it with newspapers, before sitting down to a feast of cold beer and blue crabs. On this day, however, it was just me, myself and I. Unfortunately, I was the designated driver, so I stuck to a tasty crab cake and a soft drink.

There are several small harbor marinas in Chesapeake City. Each provides mooring for millions of dollars worth of both big and small pleasure boats. Many came and went as I watched from my vantage point in the marina parking lot.

⊷ THE TANGENT POINT ⊷

SATURDAY - AUGUST 25, 1764
*". . . produced the Line till we judged we were past the Point settled before to be the
Tangent Point in the circle around New Castle of 12 Miles Radius."*

In exactly six weeks, the 81 miles, 78 chains, and 31 links (81.98 miles)
between the mid-point on the Transpeninsula Line and the tangent point on the
12-mile circle had been surveyed. Careful observation and calculation determined
that the northern terminus of the line was slightly to the west of the 12-mile
circle. Mason and Dixon's method of correction for placing final markers on the
lines they surveyed was to use an ultimate determination of location and then
calculate the necessary offset distance—to the east or west—for the Tangent Line
(north or south for the east-west line)—for each temporary marker post that was
necessary to place it directly on the intended line. In this case, a week was spent
calculating the offset distance to the east that each of the 5-mile marker posts
would have to be moved to correct the minor error that had crept in during the
course of the 82-mile survey.

The Tangent Point marker is located in the thick undergrowth between
the Iron Hill Apartments, on Iron Hill Road in Newark, Delaware and the main
line of the Penn Central Railroad. The area is very heavily overgrown. I am not
feeling particularly adventurous, and make no effort to look for the marker among
the thick mass of briars and brambles.

TUESDAY - SEPTEMBER 4, 1764
*". . .we set out on our return toward the Middle Point to make our offsets at
every 5th Mile Post as per Table marked"*

Unwilling to allow for any possibility for error, the next two months
were spent rerunning the line back to the middle point, and then back again to
the tangent point, each time calculating offsets and refining the positions of the
visible posts that mark the invisible line. At this point in time, the permanent
stone markers had arrived from England, and they were set in position, replacing
the temporary wooden posts that had been previously installed. Success at last!
Mason wrote that he was finally satisfied that the survey posts were positioned as
near as they could reasonably be "in the true Tangent Line."

TUESDAY - NOVEMBER 13, 1764

"On measuring the angle of our last line with the direction from New Castle, it was so near a right angle, that, on a mean from our lines, the above mentioned post is the true tangent point. From the whole we conclude that the offset posts in our last visto marked MD are (or as near as practible) in the true Tangent Line."

The only notation in the survey journal for the next seven days was one brief sentence: *"Waiting for the Commissioners."* The pair packed up and traveled to New Castle to meet with the commissioners of both provinces. The meeting took place at Christiana Bridge on November 21st. Its focus was to detail their efforts and report on the results of the survey and marking of the 82-mile   Tangent Line.

FRIDAY - NOVEMBER 23, 1764

"At this meeting the Gentlemen Commissioners came to a resolution that what we had done relating to the Lines should stand as finished."

Two days later, all of the hired hands were paid off and discharged. Mason and Dixon then made the 20-mile horseback ride to the Harlan Farm in Newlin Township to hide out during the cold winter months ahead.

Westward Ho

⤖ A Lesson in Spherical Trigonometry ⤖

March 1, 1765

*"Began to prepare for the running of the Western Line: the method of
proceeding as follows, Let P be the Pole, ABCD the Parallel of Latitude to be drawn
. . . At pleasure suppose = 10 minutes . . . . Hence Angle PAE = 89 degrees 55 minutes
51 seconds . . . the angle from the North Westward."*

A true parallel of latitude is a curving line that encircles the earth. The dividing line between the provinces was to be a true parallel fifteen miles south of the city of Philadelphia. The anchor point for this line would be the Post Mark'd West. The art and science of surveying consists of marking straight lines and accurate angles; thus a circle can not be directly surveyed. The techniques used by Mason and Dixon to define and mark a true parallel of latitude—a small segment of an imaginary line that circles the earth—would require a thorough understanding of how to blend together the intricacies of land surveying, astronomy and spherical trigonometry.

If you could board an airplane and fly in a perfectly straight line from the Post Mark'd West to the southwestern corner of Pennsylvania, the route would take you north of the true parallel. The beginning and end points of the journey, however, would be directly on the true parallel, but all other points on the flight path would be north of the true line of latitude. At the midpoint, the flight path would be the farthest distance from the parallel.

In the entries in his journal for March 1, 1765, Mason laid out in detail how he would go about the complex task of surveying and marking more than 200 miles of curved line that would become the southern boundary of Penn's land grant. The method he used to locate the line of latitude was to break up the several-hundred-mile, five-degree arc into a series of smaller pieces. Mason's calculations led him to the conclusion that a straight line surveyed in the direction of 89 degrees, 55 minutes, and 51 seconds from the north toward the west from any point on the dividing line of latitude would again cross the arc at a distance about eleven miles from the starting point. At the mid-point—five and a half miles along the line—if they were right on course, they would pass about seventeen feet north of the true arc.

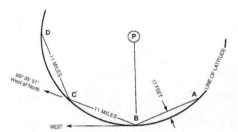

Mason's technique for surveying the circular line of latitude. By dividing the line into 11-mile segments and then making adjustments to any errors that may have crept into the task, the 18th century survey crew successfully marked the 233 miles of border with the worst error being only 700 feet.

At the eleven-mile point the survey party would halt, set up the zenith sector, and observe the stars to determine their exact location reference the curved line of latitude. The star gazing efforts would normally require at least seven clear nights, and sometimes as many as fourteen or fifteen clear nights. Once the stellar observations were completed, they could be used to compute the distance, due to error, that they were off the arc or parallel of latitude. They would then calculate the offset north or south for each of the previously measured and marked miles. The laborers could then return and move each mile marker north or south to the true boundary. This tedious procedure would be repeated for the next eleven miles.

⇢ THE BEGINNING OF THE WEST LINE ⇠

FRIDAY - APRIL 5, 1765
"Began to run the western Line in the direction of the mean of the four marks."

In the first days of April, the surveyors and their crew returned to the Post Mark'd West. They determined the direction of 4 minutes, 9 seconds north of a true west bearing, and began the survey and marking of the boundary line that would one day become a household word associated with their family names. The survey of the several-hundred-mile invisible dividing line between Pennsylvania, Maryland and what was then Virginia, was about to begin.

The survey party proceeded westward, crossing Little Christiania Creek, Great Christiania Creek and the Elk River. Using their measuring instrument—the 66-foot Gunter's Chain—a distance of 12 miles and 25 chains (12.31 miles) from the Post Mark'd West was measured. On the 16th of April they stopped. The next ten days and nights were spent taking the first of what would become a series of stellar observations. The results showed that they were 129 feet north of the true line of latitude. They planted a marker 129 feet to the south of the

The Conowingo Dam (l) and hydroelectric power plant (r) on the Susquehanna River.

observation point, and then computed the offsets for each of the other twelve mile markers. Crew members were dispatched to the east to move each marker to the south by the calculated distance.

⤙ THE SUSQUEHANNA RIVER ⤚

SATURDAY - MAY 11, 1765
"At 26 Miles 3 Chains 93 Links Reached the East side of the River Sesquehannah. Crossed the River nearly at right angles."

In the 18th century, the Susquehanna River was a meandering body of water a bit over 800 feet wide. The party moved back about 500 feet from the riverbank and set up camp. The zenith sector was set up, and for the next seventeen days the stars were observed and calculations were made to determine the position reference the true line of latitude.

Today, about five miles downstream from their 1765 camp, lies the Conowingo Dam. The waters of the Susquehanna back up behind this 105-foot-high, 4500-foot-long concrete barrier to create the Conowingo Reservoir, a manmade 14-square-mile river/lake. The waters of the river are almost a mile wide where the Mason Dixon Line crosses it.

The hydroelectric dam, operated by Exelon Generation, was constructed by the Philadelphia Electric Company between 1926 and 1928. More than 700,000 cubic yards of concrete were poured in the making of this structure. When running at full capacity, 38 million gallons of water per minute rush past the blades of the 11 turbines housed in the powerhouse on the west side of the river. This massive machinery is capable of generating 512,000 megawatts of electricity. Route 1 crosses the river on a two-lane roadway atop the structure.

⊷ LANCASTER ⊷

[Note: With nothing better to do as he waited out the snow and ice of the long Pennsylvania winter, Mason had embarked on one of his frequent "forward-exploring" junkets for nine days in January, 1765, exploring the Lancaster area. The following are his notes from that trip.]

THURSDAY - JANUARY 10, 1765

"Left Brandywine and proceeded to Lancaster (distance about 35 miles) a Town in Pennsylvania, distant from Philadelphia 75 Mile, bearing nearly West. What brought me here was my curiosity to see the place where was perpetrated last Winter the Horrid and inhuman murder of 36 Indians, Men, Women and Children, leaving none alive to tell. These poor unhappy creatures had always lived under the protection of the Pennsylvania Government and had Lands allotted for them a few Miles from Lancaster by the late celebrated William Penn, Esquire, Proprietor. They had received notice of the intention of some of the back inhabitants and had fled to the Goal (jail) to save themselves. The keeper made the door fast, but it was broken open and two men went in and executed the bloody scene ; while about 50 of their party set on Horse Back without; armed with Guns, etc. Strange as it was that the Town though as large as most Market Towns in England, never offered to oppose them, though it's more than probable they on request might have been assisted by a company of his Majesties Troops who were there in Town. . .no honor to them! What was laid to the Indians charge was that they held a private correspondence with the Enemy Indians; but this could never be proved against the men and the women and the children (some in their Mother's womb that never saw light) could not be guilty."

In the mid-1750s, Indian war parties frequently decimated the villages of white European settlers throughout the provinces of Pennsylvania and Maryland, and hundreds died by their hands. Angered by the fact that their government seemed to turn a deaf ear to their predicament, and offered little assistance for their defense, a group of citizens from the area of the Susquehanna River loaded the mutilated bodies of settlers murdered by the Indians onto open wagons and took them to Philadelphia. Here they displayed their gruesome cargo by parading it through the streets of the city for all to see. Then, in an effort to leave a lasting impression on those in a position to come to their aid, the decaying bodies were dumped on the steps of the State House.

However, the Indians had no corner on violence. Just weeks after Mason and Dixon arrived in Philadelphia, a group of self-styled toughs from Paxton, Pennsylvania attacked a small band of Conestoga Indians who had lived peaceably with the white settlers in the Susquehanna Valley for decades. The Paxton Boys, as they later became known, murdered six of the Conestogas and set their village on fire. The survivors fled into the town of Lancaster. In an effort to protect them, the sheriff locked them in the town jail, but the mob broke into the jail and murdered the men, women and children that were hiding there. Neither the townspeople nor the group of English soldiers that were in town sounded a voice or lifted a hand in protest. Encouraged by their ability to intimidate by terrorizing, the Paxton Boys pursued another group of the fleeing Indians all the way to Philadelphia. News of the bloodbath made the news headlines in the City of Brotherly Love. From Mason's note in the survey journal, we can deduce that just a bit over a year later the cruelty of the events that had taken place in Lancaster still aroused a sense of pity in the God-fearing Englishman. In mid-winter of 1765, Mason's curiosity got the best of him. He took a leave of absence from the warmth of the Harland farmhouse and journeyed to Lancaster to see for himself the site where this atrocity had been committed.

⚛ COLUMBIA ⚛

THE ALMOST CAPITOL OF THE NEW NATION

THURSDAY - JANUARY 17, 1765
". . .I fell in company with Mr. Samuel Smith who in the year 1736   was Sheriff of Lancaster County, now three counties, Lancaster, York and Cumberland, who informed me that the People near the supposed Boundary Line were then at open war. About ten miles from Lancaster on the River Susquehanna one Mr. Cresap defended his house as being in Maryland, with 14 Men, which he surrounded with about 55. They would not surrender (but kept firing out) till the House was set on fire, and one man in the House lost his life coming out."

The area around the Susquehanna River near Lancaster, in the days prior to Mason and Dixon's survey, was Thomas Cresap country. Cresap was a hot-tempered Englishman from Yorkshire who emigrated to America to seek his fortune. He eventually settled in Wrightsville, Pennsylvania about 1730 on land granted to him by the proprietors of the province of Maryland. In the early 1730s the Wright Family operated a company that transported passengers and cargo across the river, known locally as Wright's Ferry. Cresap, for a time, ran this business

The restored 18th century Wright Family Mansion is open for public tours during the summer months.

for the Wrights. The town is almost twenty miles north of the Pennsylvania-Maryland border, about midway between Lancaster and York. One would be inclined to think that land this far north of the actual border would be immune from arguments about provincial ownership.

Much to the consternation of his neighbors, Cresap, who had by then been commissioned a captain in the Maryland militia, insisted that this land was in Maryland. The series of confrontations and altercations that engulfed Cresap became known as the Conojacular War. Eventually his shenanigans led to armed conflict and the loss of life. In November 1736, he was arrested by the sheriff of Lancaster County and taken in irons to a jail in Philadelphia. When the recalcitrant Yorkshireman proclaimed, "This is the prettiest city in Maryland that I've ever seen!" In August of the following year, King George II decreed that no more land grants along the border could be made by either province. Furthermore, there were to be no more "tumults, riots, or other outrageous disorders committed along the borders." Cresap was released from prison with the proviso that he never return to Wrights Ferry. He moved his family 150 miles to the west. As we follow the story of the survey of the dividing line Cresap's name will resurface time and time again.

Columbia is the home to the National Watch & Clock Museum and the NAWCC School of Horology. The museum houses more than 12,000 clocks, watches, tools and other time related items. During the one-hour tour of the museum one literally walks through the history of time keeping, starting with the early attempts of the Egyptians to catalog the days that make up a year and ending with the atomic clock that can split seconds into pieces! The school of

Take a walk through the history of time keeping from 4000 BCE in Egypt to the Atomic Clock of the 21st century at the American Watch & Clock Museum in Columbia.

horology, which shares the campus with the museum, trains its students in the art and science of clock and watch making, repairs and restoration.

Wright's Ferry is the town that came very close to becoming the nation's capital. In 1789 Congress was debating the location of the permanent seat for the new U.S. government. Harrisburg, Lancaster, York and Germantown were in the running, along with what was then called Wright's Ferry. The town's leaders quickly changed its name to Columbia in anticipation of what they hoped would come to pass. The U.S. House of Representatives voted in favor of Columbia, but the bill to locate the national capital on the Susquehanna River lost in the Senate by one vote.

Saturday - May 25, 1765

"... about sunset I was returning from the other side of the river, and at the distance of about 1.5 Mile the Lightning fell in perpendicular streaks, (about a foot in breadth in appearance), from the cloud to the ground. This was the first Lightning I ever saw in streaks continued without the least break through the whole, all the way from the Cloud to the Horizon."

Tuesday - May 28, 1765

"Packing up the Instruments, etc."

Wednesday - May 29, 1765

"Set out on our return to lay off the offsets; and reached the 20 Mile Post"

Thursday - May 30, 1765

"Set off the offsets to the 15 Mile Post"

The North Line

⊷ THE TANGENT POINT TO THE LINE OF LATITUDE ⊷

MONDAY - JUNE 3, 1765
"Proceeded to run the North Line"

At the end of May, Mason and Dixon temporarily abandoned their efforts to push westward, and returned to the tangent point on the western border of Delaware. For the next three weeks, their efforts were directed at surveying and marking the Delaware-Maryland border from this point north to the southern border of Pennsylvania. After working out the complicated procedure to survey a curving line of latitude, a straight line in the direction of true north would be a welcome task that the surveyors could perform with ease! However, the royal charter for the lands that made up these Lower Three Counties—present-day Delaware—contained the provision that ". . . *all lands within twelve miles from the town of New Castle . . .*" would be included. Some of the land inside the twelve-mile radius was a bit west of the straight line from the tangent point running due north. To be precise, the border would be a little less than a two mile arc before beginning its straight true north run. When all was surveyed and marked, the slight bulge in the border to the west amounted to 116 feet at the middle of the arc. About five acres of land that otherwise would have ended up in Maryland was properly included as part of the Lower Three Counties of Pennsylvania. On June 3rd the party started to run the line, and completed the task of surveying and marking it in short order—three days to be exact.

"...all lands within 12 miles..." Mason was a stickler for accuracy. The 12 mile circle intrudes slightly to the west of the North Line adding about five acres to the lands that make up the state of Delaware.

The bulge in the border is so slight that you can easily miss it even when looking carefully at the NEWARK WEST 7.5 Minute USGS Quadrangle map.

Quad maps have a very large scale of 1:24,000; one inch on the map equals 2000 feet [24,000 inches] on the ground; a mile being about 2.5 inches on the map. The combination of the small arc and the straight north-south line, from the tangent point to the parallel that is fifteen miles south of Philadelphia, is just a bit over five miles.

⟶ The Wedge: No Man's Land ⟵

In 1765 this three mile meridian defining the eastern border of Maryland created no problems. What is now the state of Delaware was then the Lower Three Counties of Penn's province. The line formed the border between Pennsylvania and Maryland.

This, however, planted the seeds for a problem and a controversy that was destined to arise eleven years later. After the Declaration of Independence was signed in 1776, the Lower Three Counties not only declared themselves free of British rule, but also established a state government separate from Pennsylvania. Delaware was born, the first state in the new Union.

The borders of the first state reverted to what was described in the old charter. The northern border of the lands of Delaware now followed the arc all the way to the tangent point. This created a pie-shaped piece of land to the west of the arc and to the east of the survey line that would become a center of controversy for 125 years. Maps drawn in the 1800s displayed this as a thin tongue of Pennsylvania jutting southward between the established borders of Delaware and Maryland. It was about five miles north to south and a bit less than a mile wide on its northern edge—somewhat less than 800 acres in size. This slither of no-man's land became known as the Wedge. Cartographers assigned its ownership to Pennsylvania, but those who lived in the Wedge considered themselves citizens of Delaware, as they paid taxes and voted in Delaware. Yet official maps persisted in labeling it as part of the Commonwealth of Pennsylvania.

This ambiguousness resulted in the territory becoming a haven for bandits and associated illegal activities. Legends of wild west-type pranks were widespread. When any lawman from Delaware showed up to put a stop to gambling, dog fights, cock fights and other unlawful behavior in the area, the crowd gthered for the event would quickly produce a map and insist that they were in Pennsylvania. Conversely, when the sheriff of Chester County came on the scene, he would be accused of being in Delaware, conveniently outside the limits of his jurisdiction.

In the latter part of the 19th century, the two states appointed a joint committee charged with the task of coming up with a solution to the matter. In 1889 it recommended that the Wedge officially become part of Delaware. The decision was quickly ratified by the Pennsylvania legislature in 1897 but wasn't adopted by Delaware and United States lawmakers until 1921.

New London Road (Route 896) runs northwestward from Newark through the Wedge. The town of Mechanicsville sits astride the highway. As I drive along Route 896 I expect that I might see some remnants of the sinfulness that was rumored to have taken place in this area, but I am disappointed. Mechanicsville is a quiet bedroom-type community, and the only activity that I note on this spring morning as I pass through the Wedge is centered in a greenhouse just to the west of the highway. Here I watch as numerous flats of annual flower plants and vegetables are purchased and hauled off to be planted in the many neatly-manicured gardens in the area.

The Wedge - 800 acres of no man's land.

Across the street from the greenhouse, Hopkins Road intersects with Route 896 and runs off to the east through Walter Carpenter State Park. The area is very heavily wooded. I am searching for the Arc Corner marker - where the twelve-mile arc line that forms the northern boundary of Delaware yields to the actual beginning of the east-west Mason Dixon Line.

While the five-foot-tall Arc Corner marker is easily accessed, it can also be easily missed. I drive past it three times, keeping one eye on traffic and the other on the GPS receiver, before I recognize the spot where Hopkins Road crosses into Pennsylvania and then juts immediately back into Delaware. There are no signs that state "Welcome to Pennsylvania" or "Welcome back into Delaware". This interstate excursion is only about a hundred feet in length. It can be identified where a footpath with a barrier to keep out motorized vehicles heads off to the northwest. The tip-off for the location of the marker is a sign on the barrier that threatens dire consequences for anyone parking in the entrance way. It indicates that gendarmes from the Commonwealth of Pennsylvania will carry out enforcement of the edict! I chance it and back into the "No Parking" area, while scanning the tree line on the other side of the road. It must be here somewhere! There, immediately across from my vantage point in the "No Parking"

The ARC Cornerstone, where two of the most famous border lines in the United States intersect.

zone is the Arc Corner marker, standing guard duty in a clearing, silently watching the cars pass by from state to state on Hopkins Road. I feel a bit foolish for not having spied it in my three drive-bys, as it is hard to miss when looking directly across the road from the entrance to the footpath. At this spot, the 12-mile radius arc border of northern Delaware intersects the line of latitude surveyed and marked by Mason and Dixon. I spend a few moments enjoying the spring morning, leaning against the stone pillar that marks the junction of two of the most unique invisible lines drawn on the surface of the North American continent—the only circular border of any state in the union, the PA-DE Arc Line and the east-west Mason Dixon Line. The two surveyors and their party of workers passed by this place on Monday, April 8, 1765. The monument was installed 130 years later, in 1896.

In my travels north along New London Road I happen to sneeze. I miss the passing from Delaware, through a few hundred yard slice of Maryland and then into Pennsylvania. Within a span of less than thirty seconds, I motor through three states. The northeast corner of Maryland, where it intersects with Delaware and Pennsylvania, lies a few hundred feet to the east of the road. If one could run the clock back two-and-a-third centuries to Tuesday, April 9, 1765, a flagman might have stopped you as a certain survey party dragged a Gunter's Chain across Route 896.

Pushing the Line West

FRIDAY - JUNE 21, 1765
"Set out for the River"

SATURDAY - JUNE 22, 1765
"Reached (the river) at Peach Bottom Ferry"

With the north line now surveyed and marked, the crew set out to pick up where they left off on May 30th. After some minor course corrections, Mason and Dixon and their entourage crossed the Susquehanna River and proceeded to survey and mark the great dividing line of latitude to the west. After three weeks, they arrived at a point near where today Interstate 83 crosses the line. Here they paused to set up camp on July 12, 1765. For the next eleven days, they once again became stargazers, with clear weather prevailing for the entire period.

When their calculations were complete, they made a slight correction in their position, and on July 24th began to push west once again.

WEDNESDAY - JULY 24, 1765
"At 49 miles 7 chains crossed the lower Road leading from York to Joppa and Baltimore"

Today, in this spot described in the journal, there are two roads—the York Road on the Pennsylvania side of the line, and Maryland Route 45 to the south of the line. This two-lane, asphalt-paved conduit follows a primitive trail cut through untamed lands that led from York to Baltimore in 1765. Paralleling it, just 500 feet to the east, is a modern 21st century concrete-paved trail that is part of the U.S. Interstate Highway System.

Interstate 83 is one of the shorter interstate highways in the country, and was one of the first to be built in Pennsylvania. Construction began in 1954, but it was not until 1971 that it was finally completed. Its northern terminus is in Harrisburg, Pennsylvania at Interstate 81, and it ends just 85.3 miles southeast in Baltimore. About 37,000 vehicles cross the Mason Dixon Line each day on this interstate.

The Dobbin House, in Gettysburg, built in 1776 by the Reverend Alexander Dobbin. For twenty-five years the building served as one of the first classical schools west of the Susquehanna River. It's now a museum furnished in the motif of the late 18th century.

⟿ GETTYSBURG ⟿

SATURDAY - AUGUST 24, 1765
*"Continued the Line 79.56 Mr. John McKinley's House 2 chains South
80.21 Crossed Marsh Creek. Breadth two chains"*

It is very difficult to imagine the carnage that took place at this peaceful looking spot during the first three days of July in 1863. The bloodshed began just before sunrise on July 1, 1863 when initial shots were exchanged between Confederate and Union soldiers across Marsh Creek, just a few miles from the point where Mason and Dixon forded the rambling waters of the stream almost a century before. The last shot was fired late in the day on July 3rd, and by that time Union losses numbered approximately 23,000, while estimates of Confederate losses ranged between 20,000 and 28,000 souls. The front page of the New York Times, Saturday, July 4, 1863, carried this dispatch:

FROM THE BATTLE FIELD NEAR GETTYSBURG: TODAY, AND ON PENNSYLVANIA SOIL HAS BEEN FOUGHT ONE OF THE MOST DESPERATE AND BLOODY BATTLES OF THIS ACCURSED REBELLION.

Gettysburg, a town with just over 7000 year-round residents, is a family tourist destination. For part of the year, the population swells dramatically, and on a typical summer weekend all of the restaurants, souvenir shops and ice cream stands are packed to capacity. All of the hotels and bed and breakfasts in

"The saints eternal camping ground, their silent tents are spread; glory guards these solemn grounds; the bivouac of the dead." It was from this spot that President Lincoln delivered the Gettysburg Address(r).

town have been booked for weeks, and there are waiting lines to get inside the numerous 17th and 18th century structures that are open to the public.

Tour buses and private cars clog the narrow streets. The humanity packing the sidewalks is beginning to overflow into the streets. Bicyclists make it even more difficult for motorized vehicles to pass. The parking lots at the Gettysburg National Military Park Visitor Center are more than half-full, and it is just a few minutes before 10 a.m.

The souvenir shop in the visitor center sells all manner of memorabilia including front page replicas of old newspapers. That is how I know what the headlines were on the front page of the New York Times a century and a half ago!

My wanderings take me out of air-conditioned visitor center and across the street. The imposing gates of the Gettysburg National Cemetery are open. A wrought iron stanchion stands in the middle of the entrance road supporting a small round sign. The message is brief but concise: **SILENCE and RESPECT**. Almost level with the grass line is row after row after row of small square stones. Each is marked with a number—926, 927, 928, 929, 930. . .—and so on. Each miniature monument marks the final resting place of one of the thousands of Confederate and Union soldiers who came to do battle in Gettysburg in July of 1863, and who will remain here forever. Each is anonymous, yet never to be forgotten.

Families fill the walkways and stroll among the cannon on display. They obviously have taken the words of the sign to heart—all you can hear is the rustle of the leaves in the humid breeze of mid-morning. I pause and lean against the Soldiers National Monument, and just for a moment close my eyes and try to transport myself back a century and a half. If you concentrate, you can envision a man with a beard wearing a tall stovepipe hat. Listen carefully and you can hear the echoes of a time long gone by: "Four score and seven years ago our fathers brought forth, upon this continent, a new nation, conceived in Liberty, and dedicated to the proposition that all men are created equal." I am filled with awe, for I am standing in the very spot where Abraham Lincoln first uttered those words, four-and-a-half months after the ferocious battle that took place in the nearby fields. The focal point of the cemetery is this monument. It was dedicated in 1869, where President Lincoln delivered his now famous Gettysburg Address.

Legislation was enacted by Congress in 1895 to establish Gettysburg Memorial Park as a monument dedicated to the armies that fought a battle here that manifested what the United States of America looks like as a nation today. The park incorporates almost 6000 acres, has 26 miles of roads and hiking trails and over 4000 markers, monuments and memorials.

➵ SITE R: A SECRET NOT-SO-SECRET HIDEAWAY ➵

FRIDAY - AUGUST 30, 1765
"88 Miles 00 Chains Mr. John Chohorn's House one chain North in the South Mountain"

SATURDAY - AUGUST 31, 1765
"Continued the Line"

Had the survey crew of 90 to 100 hands been making their way through the wilderness just a bit east of the present-day village of Blue Ridge Summit on a Friday or Saturday afternoon in the 21st century, they probably would set off many alarms. They certainly would have been looked upon with great suspicion, and there is no question that they would have been the subject of careful scrutiny. There, about 1500 feet north of the survey line, at a distance of about 90 miles and 5 chains from the Post Mark'd West, is the entrance to a hollowed-out mountain. This is not your normal mountain cave, carved out by eons of water flow, but rather a man-made cave blasted out of Raven Rock Mountain with dynamite. Its official name is the Alternate Joint Communications Center— in government jargon abbreviated as the AJCC. It is also commonly known as Site R [as in Raven Rock Military Complex]. Construction of this six-story fortified communications bunker began in 1951. Its original function during the

Cold War was to be a joint military command post, to be used in the event of nuclear war. Site R has its own reservoir, sewage treatment plant and power generation plant, and is capable of housing 3000 people for extended periods of time. There is little doubt that this is where Vice President Cheney took refuge in the weeks immediately following the 911 terrorist attacks on New York and Washington.

SITE R, the end of the road. Don't strain your eyes trying to read the signs. They don't say "Welcome"!

From a distance all that I can view on the 1500-foot-high summit of Raven Rock Mountain are several communication towers. Harbaugh Valley Road, a two-lane country asphalt-paved road, leads south off PA Route 16 about two miles east of Blue Ridge Summit. There are several houses, small farms and an old country church, well-seasoned by many generations of worshippers, along the first mile or two of the road. On the east side is a two-lane, asphalt-paved entrance to a well-marked government military installation. There is no mention of Site R, but warning signs: **US GOVERNMENT PROPERTY - AUTHORIZED PERSONNEL ONLY.**

If you continue south, you eventually cross the great dividing line of latitude. However, I turn onto another country road that seems to lead up the mountain. As I round a bend, my progress is abruptly halted when a concrete Jersey barrier blocks a portion of the roadway. In addition, a substantial chain link fence topped with razor wire stops all would-be mountain explorers. On the opposite side of the barrier stands a guardhouse. All of the underbrush is cleared, and any intruder could easily be spotted from a mile away. I turn my car around and hop out to take a picture. Shortly thereafter a well-armed sentry appears, as if out of nowhere.

"Everything OK," he asks. "No problem. OK to take a picture?" was my reply. "You can do almost anything you want from your side of the fence but don't try to come over to my side!" he barked.

The genesis of the AJCC may be traced back to the late 1940s when the Soviet Union detonated its first atomic bomb, and the need for a well-protected military command center in close proximity to the nation's capital became evident. In 1950 President Truman approved the plans for the center, and construction of the facility was put on the fast track. In less than three years, the mountain had been hollowed out, and Site R was a reality.

Few individuals, other than the local residents, knew about the existence of Site R until about fifteen years ago. Today, a search of the Internet will bring up many hits on this secret/not-so-secret, government hideaway.

⚶ BLUE RIDGE SUMMIT: A COOL TOWN ⚶

TUESDAY - SEPTEMBER 3, 1765
"At 92 Miles 4 Chains Mr. George Craft's House 6 chains North in the Mountain"

Mr. George Craft and his family must have been one of the earliest inhabitants in the Blue Ridge Summit area. Charles Mason may have knocked on his door to introduce himself, or more likely Craft was curious when he noticed the better part of a hundred people walking through his fields in this remote location.

The village is indeed a cool town, situated at the pinnacle of South Mountain, about 1600 feet above sea level. It is noticeably cooler and less humid when I get out of the car to snap a picture of the old Baltimore and Ohio Railroad Station, now restored and serving as the local library. The train tracks, however, remain, and appear to be in use by freight trains. The scene conjures up childhood memories of the town in which I was born and raised. Although it was in pool-table-flat southern New Jersey, and this in the rugged mountains of central Pennsylvania, the railroad station could have easily been built from the same set of blueprints. The scenario in which the mighty steam locomotive dragged several passenger cars into the station right on time every hour was without a doubt duplicated at this very spot. As I stand next to the station, I envision the enormous steam engine grinding to a halt, still huffing and puffing from its efforts. It is easy to conjure up the acrid odor of burning coal, hear the ear-piercing hiss of steam being emitted from the engine's drive cylinders and see the thick black smoke pouring from its stack. The imagined train would not spend much time at the platform. As soon as a few folks get off, and a few others get on, the conductor standing on the lower step of one of the cars hangs onto the handrail with one hand while waving to the engineer with the other. His voice bellows out up and down the platform; "All aboard...." With that, the colossal locomotive hauls the passenger cars out of the station, and they disappear down the tracks within a few seconds. All that is left is a plume of black smoke that wafts a hundred feet into the sky.

In addition to its appearance as a quaint little village, Blue Ridge Summit's only other claim to fame is that Mason and Dixon's 233-mile-long east-west line appears to sag as far off the fifteen mile south of the city of Philadelphia latitude of the Post Mark'd West as I have yet found. The border markings between states are most noticeable not by the location of signs—they sometimes seem to be several hundred feet from the actual

The old B & O Railroad Station – now a library – at Blue Ridge Summit.

border—but by the color and type of paving marking the place where highway maintenance jurisdiction is handed off from one state to another. I straddle the two types of asphalt—the front wheels of my Tracker are in Pennsylvania and the rear wheels in Maryland. The signage here appears to be right on the mark, as I am sitting in the shadow of the **WELCOME TO PENNSYLVANIA** sign. The GPS receiver indicates that I am at N 39 degrees 43 minutes 21.5 seconds at a distance of ninety-two miles from the Post Mark'd West in Mr. Bryan's field. I am 15 miles plus 713 feet south of what was the most southern point in the city of Philadelphia in the mid-18th century. Quite accurate for a group of surveyors shooting the stars through a six-foot tube equipped with cross hairs, a plumb-bob and micrometer for determining position!

⇢ Camp #3: The Presidential Retreat ⇠

From Blue Ridge Summit I drive to a point at the summit of Catoctin Mountain, about five miles south of the ninety-two mile post. My visit to this spot is well documented by the records of the Catoctin Mountain Park Rangers.

"Keep your hands on the steering wheel and don't get out of the vehicle!" blares the loudspeaker on one of the two police cars that hem me in on the unnamed mountain road.

What a welcome to Camp David! The compound in northern Maryland is shown on USGS maps and marked on local roads as Camp #3 in Catoctin Mountain Park. President Roosevelt built this 200-acre retreat for presidents and their guests in 1942, christening it as a place "to relax and entertain." Mr.

Absent a presidential invitation, this is all you will get to see of Camp David.

Roosevelt originally named the hideaway Shangri-La, but in 1953 President Eisenhower renamed it Camp David, after his grandson. It has all the facilities of a first-class getaway for the famous and powerful. The amenities include a helicopter pad, presidential office, living quarters, guest houses, a swimming pool, a putting green and gymnasium. It is about seventy miles from Washington at the summit of Catoctin Mountain, where the 1800-foot altitude lends it natural air conditioning. Rumor has it that there is an underground tunnel between Camp #3 and Site R.

The camp has served the needs for seclusion and privacy of twelve presidents. In addition, many meetings and discussions that have changed the course of world history have been held here over the past sixty years. The planning of the Normandy Invasion, the Eisenhower-Khrushchev meetings of the 1950s and the Camp David Accords of 1978 are but a few of the historic conferences and events that have taken place on this mountain top retreat.

Don't look for a **WELCOME TO CAMP DAVID** sign. It's location is only identified as **CAMP #3** on an attractive wood-engraved sign, which further states **CLOSED TO PUBLIC**. Other signs at the entrance prohibit parking or standing, and warn that anyone passing beyond the signs will be fined. I respect the signs by not parking or getting out of the car, and resist letting my curiosity get the best of me by driving into the compound. The consequences, after all, might very well be unpleasant. Nevertheless, my physical presence and my interest obviously arouse suspicion.

"What are you doing here?" asks the ranger. "Just taking some pictures of the entrance to Camp David," I reply. "How do you know this is Camp David?" he asks.

"I typed the name into Google, the Internet search engine, and hundreds of hits came back, many identifying its location, giving directions to get here and telling the history of it. One even had photographs of this very spot!"

The ranger seems a bit perplexed. He asks for my driver's license, vehicle registration and proof of insurance, all of which he takes back to his car. Another few minutes elapse, and he then comes back to ask for my Social Security

Number. About twenty minutes after our first encounter, the ranger returns with my documents and states that I am free to go.

While the retreat itself is off limits to visitors, the rest of Catoctin Mountain Park is accessible and open to the public. Camping, fishing, picnicking and twenty-five miles of hiking trails through the hardwood forests of the park, along with the healthful atmosphere of cool, crisp mountain air, provide almost unlimited opportunities for relaxation and recreation.

THE LOST CAVE

SUNDAY - SEPTEMBER 22, 1765

"Went to see a cave (near the Mountain about 6 miles South of Mr. Shockey's) The entrance is an arch about 6 yards in length and four feet in height, where here immediately opens a room 45 yards in length, 40 in breadth and 7 or 8 in height. (not one pillar to support nature's arch.) There divine service is often (according to the Church of England) celebrated in the winter season. On the side walls are drawn by the Pencils of Time with the tears of the Rocks: The imitation of Organ, Pillar, Columns and Monuments of a Temple. which, with the glimmering faint light makes the whole an awful, solemn appearance: Striking its Visitants with a strong and melancholy reflection: That such is the abodes of the Dead: Thy inevitable doom, O stranger, soon to be numbered as one of them. From this room there is a narrow passage of about 100 yards, at the end of which runs a fine river of water. On the sides of this passage are other rooms, but not so large as the first."

Mason was once again on one of his Sunday junkets. Obviously, the sight of this beautiful creation of nature filled him with reverence and wonder—his sense of awe rings through loud and clear in his written words. The huge cavern, carved into the walls of South Mountain by water and time, somewhere near the present-day town of Smithburg, is nowhere to be found today. It has succumbed to the ravages of time and industry's efforts to extract minerals from the earth.

THE 100TH MILE STONE

MONDAY - SEPTEMBER 23, 1765
"99 miles 35 chains crossed Antietam Creek"

There is nothing special about Mile Post 100, other than its location. It is one of the many Crownstones that can be found along the Mason Dixon

Neighbors in different states.

Line. What caught my attention was its position, sitting between two mailboxes along the most nondescript of roads, not far from Hagerstown. One neighbor is in Pennsylvania; the other—right next-door—is in Maryland. Charles Mason and Jeremiah Dixon passed by here on a Monday in September 1765.

⇢ INTERSTATE 81 ⇠

THURSDAY - SEPTEMBER 26, 1765
"Continued the Line 105 miles 4 chains, Mr. Ludwig Cameron's House 4 chains north"

This location today would put the surveyors in the grassy median strip of Interstate 81, where it crosses the line. The northern terminus of the American Legion Memorial Highway, as I-81 is known, is near Watertown, New York. It follows along the spine of the Appalachian Mountains and ends 854.89 miles to the southwest at its intersection with I-40 near Dandridge, Tennessee. Construction started in the 1950s and was completed in the early 1970s. On average, 56,821 vehicles cross the Mason Dixon Line on I-81 each day.

Just south of the line, I-81 makes a sweeping turn to the west, to make way for the Washington County Regional Airport, which serves the needs of the Hagerstown area. A huge CitiBank complex is perched between the airport and Route 163, which straddles the dividing line. If you use a CitiBank VISA Card, your monthly billing statement is probably mailed to you from this aggregation of buildings, whose entrance is at Mile Post 106.

⇢ JONATHAN HAGER'S TOWN ⇠

TUESDAY - SEPTEMBER 24, 1765
101 miles 71 chains – Mr. Samuel Irwin's Spring House – 2 chains North
102 miles 34 chains – Mr. Michael Walker's House – 4 chains North
102 miles 57 chains – A great spring running into Antietam
102 mile 70 chains – Mr. William Douglas' House – 4 chains North

WEDNESDAY - SEPTEMBER 25, 1765
"Continued the Line
103 miles 5 chains - crossed road leading to Swaddingem's Ferry on Potowmack"

THURSDAY - SEPTEMBER 26, 1765
"Continued the Line
106 miles 4 chains - Mr. Ludwig Cameroon's House - 4 chains North"

FRIDAY - SEPTEMBER 27, 1765
"Continued the Line"

SATURDAY - SEPTEMBER 28, 1765
"Continued the Line
108 miles 5 chains - Crossed road leading from Carlisle to Williams Ferry on Potowmack"

The 18th century road "leading from Carlisle to Williams Ferry," as described in the survey journal notes, follows the path of the road that today stretches from Greencastle, Pennsylvania to the Potomac River. Below the dividing line it is known as Maryland State Route 63.

By the middle of the 18th century, many immigrant settlers, in pursuit of their fortunes in America, had started to move inland to escape the fast-paced life of the larger coastal cities of Philadelphia, Baltimore and Boston. From the surveyor's journal entries, it is evident that, at least by contemporary early American standards, the survey crew was entering a populated area. They were in fact just a few miles north of present-day Hagerstown, Maryland.

Jonathan Hager was a German immigrant who arrived in Philadelphia in 1727. A true New World entrepreneur, he capitalized on his talents as a blacksmith, gunsmith and fur trapper. By 1739 he had moved west and purchased 200 acres of land along the Moncacy River in Frederick County. The estate became known as Hager's Choice. Jonathan built his house from uncut field stones. Its strong construction indicated that he was aware of the dangers of country living. The structure was built over a spring; thus he had a protected water supply. The walls were twenty-two inches thick, offering protection from the forces of nature and the intrusions of unfriendly humans. It was as much a fort as a house. Today the structure stands proudly in Hagerstown's City Park. It has been completely restored, and is furnished with period pieces. An adjacent museum contains many 18th and 19th century artifacts that were unearthed

The Hager House in Hagerstown's City Park.

during the restoration project.

As time passed Hager added additional acreage to his holdings. By the mid-1760s he owned more than 2500 acres in the region. In 1762, three years before Mason and Dixon's passage through the area, he began to carve a city out of the wilderness by selling individual lots. The settlement predictably became known as Hagers-Town.

Where people gather industry will follow. During the decade after Jonathan Hager founded his town, the Catoctin Iron Furnace began to operate. It produced pig iron from the hematite ore mined from the mountain of the same name. The furnace, located east of Hagerstown, was fueled with charcoal from the extensive Maryland forests. Later, coal was used to satisfy the furnace's appetite for fuel. At its peak of production, hundreds of workers were employed—wood cutters, miners who dug the ore, founders who operated the furnace and molders who cast the hot iron into the finished products that were offered for sale.

A hundred years after Hager's time, in the countryside about twenty miles south of his fortified house, near the village of Sharpsburg, the earth was dyed red with the blood of thousands of soldiers. Here lies the site of the bloodiest day of the Civil War. On September 17, 1862, the army of Confederate General Robert E. Lee clashed with the troops led by Union General George McClellan in the Battle of Antietam. When casualties were finally tallied, 23,000 people were counted as dead, wounded or missing in action.

⚬ BLAIR VALLEY ROAD: THE LAST 1765 CAMP SITE ⚬

Mason's entry in the journal for Friday, the 4th of October, indicated that the survey party was at the foot of North Mountain, at a distance of 115 miles 42 chains. There is no mountain by that name on contemporary USGS maps anywhere in the vicinity. At this distance from the Post Mark'd West the party was just below the 1000 foot level of the 1500 foot plus ridge of Powell Mountain. The local typography leaves little doubt about the location of the survey party's camp, as there are but a few acres of flat terrain in the surrounding area. They were about to enter into some very rugged territory. In general, the successive ridges of the Alleghenies in this vicinity run from northeast to southwest. Within the next mile of the survey they would have to cross over the 1500 foot ridge of Rickard Mountain, then a mile after that the 1600 foot ridge of Sword Mountain, followed by the 1900 foot ridge of Two Top Mountain, and lastly the nearly 2000 foot ridge of Bullskin Mountain.

MONDAY - OCTOBER 7, 1765
"Set up the Sector in our Direction at the Distance of 117 miles 12 chains 97 links from the Post marked West in Mr. Bryan's Field .."

One event that is documented beyond any doubt is the location of their last encampment in 1765. It was in the Blair Valley, on the banks of Little Conocheague Creek, a little less than five miles north of Clear Spring, Maryland. About a mile from the site, as I travel along Blair Valley Road, I come upon an Eastern box turtle struggling to make his way east across the road. I feel sorry for the poor creature. I stop the car, get out, and pick him up. He immediately goes into the protective mode, tightly closing his shell. I put him down a few feet into the grass on the east side of the road, having accomplished my good deed for the day.

The site of the last stargazing efforts of 1765 sits at 800 feet above sea level. The ridges are less than a mile on either side, looming at an altitude of more than 1500 feet. The stargazers spent sixteen nights lying on the ground, looking through the zenith sector at the stars, while making calculations to determine their true position relative the parallel of latitude they are surveying and marking.

To the immediate west of the road, the terrain falls off into Little Conocheague Creek. To the east there is a level plot of ground that stretches out for several hundred feet. This must have been the site of the camp. My adrenaline always runs high when I visit one of the camp sites. I am always hoping to find something unusual, perhaps some artifact from activities that occurred in an age long past. Thus far, I have been disappointed, and this visit proves to be no exception. About ten feet off the road, where the asphalt changes from light to dark, is a wood-engraved sign supported on two short poles: **MASON AND DIXON LINE - STARGAZERS STONE**. The only stargazer's stone that I am aware of was way back in Embreeville, on the Harland Farm. The USGS map does, however, indicate that Mile Post 117 is just to the east of the road, perhaps under the sign. I walk through the knee-high weeds in search of it, finding no stone, but instead a rather large curled up black snake, no doubt lying in wait for a tasty rodent to pass by. After all, it is lunch time. I immediately yield the territory to him and retreat to my car.

On my way back into Clear Spring I once again see my friend the turtle, but this time he's a sad sight. Having obviously changed his mind and decided to come back across the road and journey to the west, he was no match for a passing car. He is but a spot on the black asphalt.

⇒ ANOTHER SUNDAY JUNKET ⇐

SUNDAY - SEPTEMBER 29, 1765
"At the River Potowmack - Forded it above the Ferry; here the Conecocheague falls into said River about seven miles to the south of our line - On the Virginia side is a log fort and a tavern. The River is about 200 yards wide."

Here, once again, is evidence of Mason's wanderings about the countryside on his day of rest. His explorations took him on horseback to the banks of the Potomac River, where he discovered a tavern on the Virginia side. No doubt he indulged in some of the good food and drink available at the inn, a pleasant respite from the chow wagon food served up by the survey party cooks.

⇒ CAPTAIN EVAN SHELBY, JR. ⇐

FRIDAY - OCTOBER 25, 1765
"Went to Captain Shelby's to desire him to go with us on the North Mountain for him to show us the course of the River Potowmack Westward."

SATURDAY - OCTOBER 26, 1765
"Repaired with Captain Shelby to the Summit of the Mountain in the direction of our Line, but the air was so hazy prevented our seeing the course of the River."

SUNDAY - OCTOBER 27, 1765
"Capt. Shelby again went with us to the summit of the Mountain (when the air was very clear) and showed us the Northernmost bend of the River Potowmack at the

Conoloways; from which we judge the line will pass about two miles to the North of the said River. From hence we could see the Allegany Mountains for many miles, and judge it by its appearance, to be about 50 miles distance. . ."

Lord Baltimore's grant specified the western boundary of Maryland as the **"...*true meridian of the first fountain of the river Potowmack, thence verging to the south, unto the further bank of the said river, and following the same on the west and south* . . .".** Once the origin of the Potomac River was located, it would seem to leave little ambiguity as to the western and southern boundary line of Maryland. However, as evidenced from this entry in their field notes, the surveyors had some concern that the northern hook of the Potomac River might lay north of their line of latitude. If this were the case, matters would be greatly complicated. The boundary between Maryland and Virginia was the Potomac. The southern boundary of Penn's land grant was defined as a constant line of latitude. If the line intersected the river, Maryland would be divided into two unconnected parcels of land, with a portion of Virginia forming an awkward bulge into southern Pennsylvania. Before calling it quits to wait out the 1765-1766 winter, Mason was anxious to have an advance glimpse of what difficulties he might encounter when work resumed the following spring. They enlisted Captain Shelby to take them to the top of North Mountain for a glimpse of what would lie ahead.

This way to Captain Shelby's House.

Evan Shelby, Jr. was born in Tregaron, Cardiganshire, Wales in 1714. He emigrated to America with his parents in 1719, the family settling first in Pennsylvania and later in Washington County, Maryland. He eventually acquired a vast tract of 24,000 acres of land near North Mountain.

Shelby was no stranger to the frontier wilderness of the New World. He served during Braddock's campaign in 1755, and was later commissioned as a captain of a company of Maryland Rangers. Captain Shelby was straight forward and very aggressive in both civilian and military affairs. In addition to his pursuit of various enterprises, he served as a Maryland magistrate during Mason and Dixon's time period.

Their surveying fears were unfounded. The Potomac River flowed just below the dividing line of latitude—but just barely. One of their estimates of

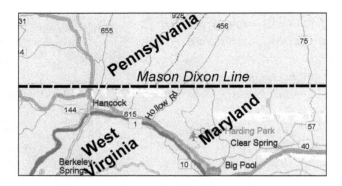

From the summit of North Mountain Mason was able to see the northern hook of the Potomac River. It was evident that the dividing line would lie about two miles north.

distance was exceedingly accurate. Today, the village of Hancock, Maryland is situated in this two-mile-wide neck of land between the Mason Dixon Line and the Potomac River. Their other estimate was a bit off the mark. Sidling Hill—the first high ridge of the Allegany Mountains to the west—is about thirty-five miles from their observation point on North Mountain.

On October 28th work on the line was terminated for the season at the foot of North Mountain. The distance to the post marked west in Mr. Bryan's field was 117 miles. The party ascended the mountain to get a view of the country beyond. They then turned to the east, marking the offsets that completed the curved line of latitude.

TUESDAY - APRIL 1, 1766
*"Changed the Direction found by the stars on the 21st and 22nd of October last . . .
and continued the Line in the Direction so changed"*

THURSDAY - APRIL 3, 1766
"At 118 miles 63 chains crossed the Head of Little Licking Creek"

FRIDAY - APRIL 4, 1766
"Continued the Line. At 119 miles 18 chains (The summit of the North Mountain)"

The field season of 1766 began on April 1st. The survey crew gathered at the spot on the east slope of North Mountain where they had dispersed five months previously. In the general area indicated by the survey journal the various peaks in the extremely rough terrain can be identified as Cross Mountain, Bullskin Mountain, Bear Pond Mountain, Sword Mountain and Hearthstone Mountain. Their April 4th location of 119 miles 18 chains from the Post Mark'd West put them at the second peak of Two Top Mountain. This 1800 foot ridge swoops down from the northeast across the dividing line a half-mile into Maryland, before abruptly changing course to run northwest back into Pennsylvania. The steep walled V-shaped valley, appropriately indicated as The Punch Bowl on the map, is about 900 feet in elevation. Little Licking Creek runs along the floor of this valley.

THURSDAY - APRIL 17,1766
"At 121 miles 61 chains crossed a Road leading from Fort Frederick to the little cove"

The rough terrain and damp weather, in the form of rain and snow, hampered progress for the next two weeks. The journal entry at 121 miles 61 chains made on April 17th indicates that they were only a little over two miles from their location of almost two weeks ago. A 21st century map shows a light duty road, Little Cove Road, leading from the tiny village of Yeakle Mill, south across the dividing line.

Fort Frederick, once a safe haven in the wilderness from Indian attack, is now a must-see for visitors to this part of Maryland.

⟫ FORT FREDRICK ⟪

FRIDAY - APRIL 4, 1766

"Fort Fredrick in Maryland is nearly south Distant about 8 miles and Fort Louden (under Parnell's Nob in Pennsylvania) nearly North, Distant about 11 miles. At 117 miles 47 chains crossed the first Spring running into the Big Licking Creek which is on the West side of the North Mountain"

Here I go venturing into another park, hoping that I don't have a repeat of my experience in Catoctin Mountain Park. Fort Frederick is located to the south of Route 70, a few miles east of Hancock. Today I am the only one inside the visitor's center, so I have a very pleasant conversation with the woman who both tends the store and answers questions. She invites me to watch the ten-minute video which tells the story of the fort. The lights dim and the presentation begins.

Fort Frederick has been here since 1756. It was here when the survey party passed nearby, about eight miles to the north. The unusually large stone-walled fort was literally built by Governor Horatio Sharpe to protect the outlying frontier settlers against Indian attack. It also served as a supply depot for military operations in the western Maryland frontier. Sharpe was a hands-on kind of governor; he personally took part in the construction of the stone walls that encircled the fort. He was criticized by the legislature for the choice of high-priced stone over less expensive wood stockade construction, but Sharpe had heard of the Indians burning down the wood forts in Pennsylvania, and he wanted no such destruction here in his province. The fort was named after Frederick Calvert, the Lord Proprietor of Maryland. In 1758, when the British won the French and Indian War, the danger on the frontier seemed to be over, and

Fort Frederick was abandoned. However, the peace was short lived. In 1763 the Ottawa Indian Chief Pontiac forged an alliance with numerous tribes in the area, and led massive raids against the land-hungry European colonists. Fort Frederick was reopened for a time, serving as a refuge for 700 settlers. The British put down the Indian uprising, and the area around Fort Frederick once again became a peaceful farming community. Later, during the Revolutionary War, the fort served as a prison camp. After the war, the fort was once again decommissioned, and by the early 20th century it was but a pile of rubble. The state acquired it in 1923 and it became one of Maryland's first state parks. Today, it has been totally restored to its original 18th century appearance, a fitting reminder of its place in history.

⊷ HANCOCK, MD ⊷

THURSDAY - APRIL 24, 1766
"At 129 3/4 miles by estimation the Northernmost bend of the River Potowmack - bore South distant about a mile and a half"

Europeans first settled in this area of Maryland about thirty-five years prior to the visit by Mason and Dixon. Their outpost was called Tonoloway Settlement. Charles Polke was the most prominent of the "Indian Traders of the Potomac" who were active in this area. His great-grand-nephew, James Polk, would one day become the 11th president of the United States. Polk's trading post was located just to the south of West Main Street, in the present-day village of Hancock.

Edward Hancock operated a ferry that carried passengers and light cargo across the Potomac River. When the Revolutionary War broke out, Hancock abandoned his ferry business and enlisted in the 8th Pennsylvania Regiment. Over the years, Tonoloway Settlement became known as Hancock.

The Chesapeake and Ohio Canal arrived in Hancock in 1839, bringing plenty of industry to the river town. During the digging of the canal, magnesium limestone was discovered a few miles west of the city. Shaffer's Cement Mill was built on the site of this discovery, beginning operation in 1839. By 1860, the mill was Hancock's largest employer. It was renamed the Round Top Hydraulic Cement Company after being sold in 1863. A water wheel drove four pairs of five-foot-diameter grindstones. There were also eight coal-fired kilns. The finished product was packed into 300-pound barrels and 100-pound sacks for shipment by canal boat to eastern markets. By the dawn of the 20th century, natural cement

The century-and-a-half-old C & O Canal as it appears today in Hancock, Maryland. The restored Bank Road Tollhouse.

had been replaced by the slower-setting and stronger Portland Cement. The mill produced its last barrel of cement in 1909, but ruins of its eight kilns can be seen from the towpath of the old C & O Canal.

By the middle of the 19th century, several arteries of transportation converged in or near Hancock. Cumberland and Wheeling were connected early in the 1800s by the National Road. Travel to the east of Cumberland, however, was still via unimproved trails. In order to take advantage of the major road to the west, commercial interests advocated that a road be built that would connect Hagerstown and Cumberland. Several financial organizations were enticed to bankroll the formation of the Cumberland Turnpike Company in exchange for an extension of their charters. The involvement of banking interests caused the road to become commonly known as the Bank Toll Road. Eventually the improved highway was extended to connect Baltimore with Cumberland.

A restored Bank Road tollhouse sits on the north side of Maryland Route 144 just west of Hancock. A schedule of tolls for everything from the movement of cattle across the road to a single man on a horse is posted on the side of the building.

The combination of the canal and the toll road, the B & O Railroad on the Virginia side of the river, and its importance as a north-south river crossing made Hancock a target for opposing armies during the Civil War. In January 1862, the city came under assault from the 8500-man army of General Thomas "Stonewall" Jackson. Union forces from Hagerstown and Cumberland came to the defense of Hancock and turned back the Confederate offensive. However, before withdrawing to Winchester, Jackson's army raided a supply train and carted off a half-million dollars worth of material. In July 1864, when the Confederate armies returned. Hancock was pillaged and burned.

After the war, the town once again prospered as a commercial center. Toward the end of the 19th century, a bridge was built over the Potomac River, connecting Hancock with the new state of West Virginia. In the early 1900s the tracks of the Western Maryland Railroad came to the city, bringing even more commercial activity to the town that was once known as Tonoloway Settlement.

⤙ INTERSTATE 70 ⤚

THURSDAY - APRIL 24, 1765
"Continued the line - at 129 3/4 miles by estimation the northern most bend of the River Potowmack. At 130 miles 48 chains Mr. Edward Coombs House 10 chains north"

Mason's estimation of distance from the northern-most bend of the Potomac River was right on the mark. Had Mr. Coombs house still been standing two centuries later, the government probably would have acquired it by right of eminent domain as part of the Interstate 70 right-of-way. On the other hand, had the highway existed on April 24, 1766, flagmen would have had to stop traffic on the north and southbound lanes while some of the survey party hauled their Gunter's Chain across it. Standing in the grassy median Mason could have been making the above journal entry.

Travelers on I-70 experience a broad cross-section of Americana as they make their way from west to east through desert country, over the lofty peaks of the Rocky Mountains, across the rangeland and grain land of the mid-west, across the mighty Mississippi, up and over the Appalachians and then on to one of the large east coast cities. The 2175 miles of concrete that make up this thoroughfare begin at Interstate 15 in Cove Fort, Utah, then continue on to touch the cities of Denver, Kansas City, St. Louis, Indianapolis, Columbus and Wheeling before ending at a Park & Ride lot just outside Baltimore. As it makes its way across the North American continent, it traverses ten states, making I-70 one of the America's longest interstate highways.

Interstate 70 is common to the Pennsylvania Turnpike from New Stanton to Breezewood. It then leaves the toll road and makes it way south for about thirty miles to where it crosses the Mason Dixon Line, 130 miles from the Post Mark'd West. After passing into Maryland, it immediately intersects with I-68, before turning abruptly east once again for 93 miles to its eastern terminus.

⟐ INTERSTATE 68 - SIDELONG HILL ⟐

SATURDAY – APRIL 26, 1766
"Continued the line. At 134 miles, 54 chains, the foot of Sidelong Hill.
(Here we could proceed no farther with the wagons.)"

Up to this point, the survey crew had relied on horse-drawn wagons to transport equipment and supplies. In their notes, they documented their arrival at the eastern foot of Sidelong Hill, a ridge that proved to be the end of the luxury of transportation by beast and wagon. This point of decision is near where Rice Road crosses the dividing line. It can be accessed by taking Route 144 west out of Hancock. Unfortunately, the only things of interest to be seen here are some valves associated with the gas pipeline that runs fifty feet north of the dividing line for more that 100 miles.

The National Freeway—Interstate 68—could easily be known as The Mason Dixon Freeway. The highway closely hugs the dividing line for its entire 116 mile length from Hancock, Maryland to Morgantown, West Virginia. One of its closest encounters with the line is where it makes its way through Sidling Hill, a few miles west of Hancock.

Sidling Hill is a mountain ridge that originates in West Virginia and extends northeastward for about seventy-five miles through Maryland and on into Pennsylvania. The Native Americans that occupied the area once called it Sidelong Hill, but due to a typographical error in the 1800s it became known as Sidling Hill, and the name has stuck. In the early part of the 20th century, logging camps dotted the mountain ridge for as far as the eye could see. During WWII, a camp on the western side of the ridge was used to house high-value German prisoners of war.

The top of the ridge of Sidling Hill, at the point where I-68 crosses it, is about 1700 feet above sea level. During the design phase of the highway project, engineers determined that the grade of a road crossing over the top of this mountain would be too steep. A 340-foot-deep, 810-foot-long, V-shaped wedge was gouged out of the rock to accommodate the four lanes of the interstate. This man-made pass is less than a quarter mile south of the dividing line of latitude. Ten-million tons of rock was removed from the mountain, and the stone rubble was used to construct the inclined road grades that led up to the pass. The ancient exposed rock layers predate the dinosaurs by a hundred-million years. Modern highway equipment, along with five-million dollars in dynamite, took just two years to slice through the ridge of the mountain. In the process, to the delight of local rock hounds, thousands of millennia of geological rock formation were exposed.

A four-story visitor center sits adjacent to the westbound lanes of the highway at the base of the cut. The pedestrian bridge over the interstate links a parking lot, accessible from the eastbound lanes, to the center. The sight of the exposed cut on a bright, sunlit day is breathtaking. At the top of the V are the youngest rocks, primarily

The man-made mountain pass through Sideling Hill.

sandstone, followed by a seam of coal that overlies layers of softer sandstone and crumbling shale. Water constantly seeps from these rocks that once formed an ancient sea bed. The sea itself was folded into the Appalachian Mountains two-hundred-forty-million years ago. Evaporating water causes iron oxide to be deposited on the rock, imparting a red coloration to the outcrop. During the winter, an ice cascade is formed as the flowing water freezes, and when struck at a right angle by the sun's rays the mountain cut appears to be made of crystal. On a clear day, if you look to the east of this mammoth cut through the mountain from the visitor center, your view can extend for fifty miles.

⟤ WILLS CREEK MOUNTAIN ⟣

SATURDAY - MAY 31, 1766

"At 159 miles 79 chains The summit of Wills Creek Mountain: Here by estimation of some who live near the place, Fort Cumberland bears South, distant between 5 and 6 miles. At 161 miles 25 chains crossed Wills Creek. The creek in general about 30 yards in breadth, and at this time 1.5 or 2 feet nearly in depth."

Wills Mountain derives its name from a Native American known as Will who made friends with the early settlers while assisting them in mastering the ways of wilderness living. The mountain is a ridge with peaks that approach 2400 feet above mean sea level (AMSL). It runs northeast from the town of Cumberland across the Mason Dixon Line into Pennsylvania. Wills Creek originates on the mountain, and flows more or less in a southerly direction

Wills Creek at its junction with the Potomac River. No longer the wild and free flowing mountain stream, but now a waterway tamed and controlled by modern technology.

before emptying into the north branch of the Potomac River at the 1760 site of Fort Cumberland. For more than 2000 years people have inhabited this area, and as a result artifacts dating back to before the time of Christ are still found in the vicinity. In the 18th century, the creek was no doubt a vibrant, fast-flowing mountain stream that teemed with native fish. Today, as it makes its way toward the Potomac, it has been tamed for flood control purposes. The last few miles of the waterway are channeled into a concrete trough. The water appears muddy, uninviting and littered with debris as it passes the historic section of Cumberland at its confluence with the Potomac River.

At mile 162 from the Post Mark'd West, Maryland Route 35/Pennsylvania Route 96 travels the narrow valley nestled between the 2000-foot ridges of Wills Mountain and Little Allegheny Mountain. Wills Creek shares the 750-feet-above-sea-level valley floor with the highway and the tracks of the Baltimore and Ohio Railroad. The town of Ellerslie, population 1500, lies on the Maryland side of the border. The dividing line passes just beyond the back yards of the homes on the north side of Mason Dixon View—a residential street that runs off to the west of the main north-south route.

On the west side of the roadway, in Ellerslie, is the Redeemer United Church of Christ. To say the least it is a most unusual structure—not as much by its construction as by its location. As I drive by I have to take a second look. It appears as if the church itself straddles the Mason Dixon Line! I turn around, pull into the parking lot, and walk over to the 1902 resurvey marker in the middle of the front lawn. I place the GPS receiver directly on the top of the monument. Mile Post 162 is at 39 degrees 43 minutes 22.7 seconds north latitude—about 450 feet north of the Post Mark'd West in Mr. Bryan's field. Indeed, the dividing line does bisect the church. I get down on the ground to take a photograph of the marker with the church in the background.

The original structure was built in 1894 on the Pennsylvania side of the line, and was used as a Presbyterian house of worship until late in the 20th

Is this an optical illusion or is it for real? On which side of the Mason Dixon Line is the Redeemer United Church of Christ? The north side, the south side, or both?

century. In 1959, the congregation added the Sunday School building on the south side of the border. Both structures are connected through an enclosed interstate walkway. It's not an optical illusion: The south wing of the church is in Maryland and the north wing in Pennsylvania.

During the two-and-a-half-month work season the line was extended from the eastern slope of North Mountain to the valley west of Little Allegheny Mountain—a distance of about 50 miles. Here, at the foot of Savage Mountain, 165 plus miles from the Post Mark'd West, the survey party stopped on June 5, 1766. The zenith sector was brought to the site and erected just beyond the North Branch of Jennings Run. Stellar observations were made until June 17th.

The town of Wellersburg, Pennsylvania is just north of the point where Mason and Dixon stopped their work for the year 1766. The line is prominently marked by a six-foot-tall stone monument that stands on the eastern side of Maryland Route 47/Pennsylvania Route 160. It was installed by the Pennsylvania Department of Transportation and stands on the edge of the parking lot of the— appropriately named—Mason-Dixon Furniture Store.

On Thursday, June 19, 1766 the crew packed up and proceeded east. For the remainder of the season they backtracked and hacked out a vista—which they refer to in their notes as a "*visto*"—about twenty-five feet wide, centered on the true line markers, along the actual boundary line between the two provinces. Late in September, the cutting was completed back to the northeast corner of Maryland.

The Emmanual Episcopal Church now stands on the spot that Fort Cumberland once occupied in the 18th century (l). In the 18th century a parade ground – In the 21st century a city street (r).

⇥ FORT CUMBERLAND ⇤

SUNDAY - JUNE 22, 1766

"Went to see Fort Cumberland: It is beautifully situated on a rising ground, close to the Northwest fork made by the falling in of Wills Creek into the Potowmack; the Fort is in bad repair; has in it at present only 10 Six Pounders. Going to the Fort I fell into General Braddock's Road, which he cut through the Mountains to lead the Army under his command to the Westward in the year 1755; but fate; how hard: made through the desert a path, himself to pass; and never; never to return."

Early European explorers, as they arrived in the late 1720s, found a Shawnee Indian village located where Wills Creek empties into the Potomac. In 1744, the Maryland Legislature purchased the land in this area from the Shawnees, and by 1750 the Ohio Company had established a trading post at this site. A few years later, recognizing the need for a western outpost, a joint effort by the British Army and the militias of Maryland and Virginia established Fort Cumberland. The site of the old fort is on the land at the northwest confluence of the creek and the river. For about a decade 175 soldiers defended it. It was then partially abandoned in the 1760s and allowed to deteriorate, as documented in Mason's eyewitness observations in June, 1766. By the 1790s only the ruins of the fort remained.

Fort Cumberland served as a supply point for the survey party as they proceeded west. There are numerous entries in the journal that reference men and supplies being sent to the group from this outpost. In 1787 the Maryland

Legislature put its stamp of approval on the settlement by officially establishing the city of Cumberland.

Just to the south of the city, the Potomac River takes a sharp jut to the north to meet Wills Creek. This thrusts a part of the town of Ridgeley, West Virginia into the heart of the downtown area of the city.

Today, the remains of Fort Cumberland lie beneath the Episcopal Church on Washington Street, just to the west of Wills Creek. Signs posted near the church describe the contours of the old fort. Colonel George Washington's 1754-1755 log cabin office still remains, but has since been moved from its original location to Riverside Park, on Greene Street.

The eight-yard-wide vista—or "visto" as Mason termed it—cut through the wilderness by the survey crew to mark the line of latitude. This example is cut and maintained by bulldozers and brush cutters along the pipeline owned by the Columbia Gas Company. The line runs about 50 feet inside of Pennsylvania for more than 100 miles along the line. Yellow capped markers are a colorful indicator of the buried pipeline.

THURSDAY - SEPTEMBER 25, 1766

"From any Eminence in the Line, where 15 or 20 miles of the Vista can be seen, (of which there are many,) the said Line, or Vista, very apparently shows itself to form a parallel of Northern Latitude. The Line is measured Horizontal: the Hills and Mountains with a 16 1/2 Feet Level. And, besides the Mileposts we have set Posts in the true Line (mark'd W on the West side) all along the Line opposite the Stationary Points where the Sector and transit Instruments stood. The said Posts stand in the middle of the Visto; which in general is about 8 yards wide. The Number of Posts set in the West Line is 303"

➡ THE C & O CANAL ⬅
AN 18TH CENTURY ENGINEERING MARVEL

In 1785 George Washington founded the Potowmack Canal Company. The objective of the new enterprise was to improve and extend navigation on the Potomac River. A series of skirting canals were constructed around its Great Falls and the channel was deepened. The Potowmack Canal Company was the forerunner of the C & O Canal Company.

WASHINGTON, D.C. - JULY 4, 1828 - PRESIDENT JOHN QUINCY ADAMS BROKE GROUND TODAY FOR THE "GREAT NATIONAL PROJECT" - A CANAL THAT WILL STRETCH FROM THE MOUTH OF THE POTOMAC RIVER, ON THE CHESAPEAKE BAY AT GEORGETOWN, NEAR WASHINGTON, DC TO THE OHIO RIVER IN PITTSBURGH. IT IS ESTIMATED THAT THE **460** MILE-LONG CANAL WILL TAKE **10** YEARS TO BUILD AND WILL COST APPROXIMATELY **3** MILLION DOLLARS.

The estimate of time and money, even in 1828 figures, was overly optimistic, to say the least. The canal builders stopped working twenty-two years later. At that point thirteen-million dollars have been spent, but only 185 miles of the canal had been completed. Nevertheless, on October 10, 1850, a great ceremony was held in Cumberland to officially celebrate the opening of the waterway. Unfortunately, the willpower and the funds to complete the construction of the canal all the way to Pittsburgh had long since faded.

The canal was obsolete even before it opened. The same day in 1828 that President Adams turned the first shovel of dirt over to signify the beginning of the digging of the ditch and the building of the locks that would make up its infrastructure, construction commenced to extend the B & O Railroad from Baltimore to Cumberland. The rails of the iron horse arrived in Cumberland eight years before the waters of the canal.

Nonetheless, the construction of the 184.5-mile-long canal was an extraordinary engineering accomplishment. In addition to the digging of the waterway, it required the construction of 11 stone aqueducts to carry it over creeks and rivers, more than 200 culverts to allow smaller streams to pass under it, 7 dams along the Potomac River and 74 lift locks to raise the canal boats from sea level at Georgetown to 600 feet above sea level at Cumberland. The locks were 100 feet long, 15 feet wide and 16 feet deep—just spacious enough to accommodate a 95-foot-long, 14-foot-wide flat-bottomed 19th century canal boat.

For most of its path, the canal closely paralleled the Potomac River. However, in order to bypass a six-mile, twisting, curving section of the river known as the Paw Paw Bends, engineers decided that a six-tenths mile, brick-lined tunnel bored through a mountain would be the viable alternative. Again, original estimates of time and cost proved to be way off the mark. The two years of planned construction turn into fourteen years, and the original $33,500 cost

The remnants of the C & O Canal at the Cumberland end of its 185 mile trek from the Chesapeake Bay at Georgetown.

ballooned to $600,000. At times, work slowed or ground to a complete halt, due to labor disputes and lack of funds. When completed, however, the tunnel was the largest and most impressive feat of engineering expertise on the waterway.

Profitability for the canal was slow in arriving. Seasonal floods regularly damaged the infrastructure, and the Civil War brought threats to commerce on the canal. However, in 1870, it began to prove its worth, when more than a million tons of freight was moved by the C & O, as coal, building materials, lumber and flour were transported to the populated east from the mills, mines and farms of western Maryland.

In 1889 a destructive flood left the canal inoperative, and traffic was stalled for more than eighteen months. In the interim, the canal company went bankrupt and the B & O Railroad took over receivership. It was all downhill from that point on. When another flood hit in 1924, the canal was put out of business forever.

Today, many of the remnants of this important piece of American history have been restored for another generation to view, and experience what life was like along the C & O in its heyday. The towpath along the canal is now a hiking trail that extends for many miles. In some places water remains in the canal; in others it is just a dry depression in the earth, reminiscent of times long past. An adventurous person can stroll through the 3000-foot-plus brick-lined Paw Paw Tunnel, and in a small way experience the sounds, smells and sights of what it was like to travel this route in almost complete darkness on an 18th century canal boat being pulled by a pair of horses or mules.

The first floor of the visitor's center, at Canal Place, in the Queen City Railroad Station, located in the historic area of Cumberland, houses the C & O

Canal Museum, where a plethora of photographs, pictures and artifacts are on display. A ten-minute video transports the visitor back 150 years, to a time when a trip from Washington to Pittsburgh took weeks rather than hours. In those days, traveling was only for the stout-hearted. Following a 185-mile ride on the canal boat to Cumberland, one would then transfer to a stagecoach for the two day, 150-mile trip over the bumpy National Road and across the Mason Dixon Line to the western reaches of Pennsylvania.

THE WESTERN MARYLAND SCENIC RAILWAY

As a symbol of its power and prestige, the Western Maryland Railway commissioned the construction of the magnificent red-brick structure known as the "Queen City Station." It sits on the east bank of Wills Creek in the shadow of the old Fort. Today, the handsomely restored building houses the C & O Canal Museum on the first floor, and both the Allegany County Visitor & Information Center and the Western Maryland Scenic Railroad Station on the second floor.

In an effort to compete with the monopoly of the Baltimore & Ohio Railroad, the State of Maryland chartered the Western Maryland Railroad in 1853. During the next fifty years, tracks were laid from Baltimore to the north and then to west along the Mason-Dixon Line.

At the dawn of the 20th century, the line came under the control of the Gould family railroad empire. The family patriarch, George Gould, had aspirations of assembling a transcontinental railroad system, and the Western Maryland Railroad would make an ideal eastern terminus for such a system. With a new infusion of cash, the rails of the WMR finally arrived in Cumberland in 1906. Unfortunately, due to the high construction costs of the many tunnels and bridges necessary to bring the system through the rugged mountains of western Maryland, the Goulds went bankrupt. When they emerged from bankruptcy in 1910, the railroad became known as the Western Maryland Railway. Over the next half-century, the operations of the WMRY were slowly merged into the Chessie System. Eventually, the WMRY, as a separate entity, slowly disappeared, and in 1975 its last train ran west on the rails from Hancock to Cumberland.

Suddenly, as I ascend the two-dozen steps from street level to the platform of the Queen City station, the ear-shattering screech of a steam whistle pierces the tranquil air of the historic district of the city. No longer do I have to use my imagination to create memories of a half-century ago, as I did at Marydel and Blue Ridge Summit. Here, right before my eyes, is a real live, enormous,

3500 horsepower, 2-8-0 coal-fired, steam-driven locomotive making its way from Ridgeley, West Virginia, across the Potomac River, under the Interstate 68 bridge and into the station on Track 1. Thick black smoke belches from its stack, and a pure white plume of steam bellows forth from the whistle as it sounds a warning to bystanders of the approach of this behemoth of early 20th century technology. All 150 or so of us lingering on the platform

The century-old restored Queen City Railroad Station.

share the same sense of excitement, awe and anticipation. We are about to be treated to a ride on the Iron Horse of old.

The 1916 vintage Baldwin locomotive, Number 734—nicknamed *Mountain Thunder*—was originally used for freight service on various railroads in the Midwest. Eventually, it was retired and rested for many years on display as a monument to "time was" in the Illinois State Railroad Museum. In 1992, the Western Maryland Scenic Railroad—a line resurrected from the ashes of the old WMRY—purchased it. *Mountain Thunder* was carefully restored and placed back into service the next year.

The loudspeaker on the platform blasts out a warning: "Please stand back behind the yellow line!"

The ground quakes and the tracks creak under the two-hundred-fifty tons of iron as it creeps past the gathered mass of old and young admirers, all anxiously waiting to board one of the numerous passenger coaches it is dragging behind it. The radiant heat of the boiler, the heartbeat of the steam cylinders and the smell of acrid coal smoke rekindles memories of times past for the older "kids" such as myself. The youngsters stand silently, and stare in wonder and awe. The eyes of a little boy next to me are as big as silver dollars as he tightly clutches his father's hand. The driver, commander of *Mountain Thunder*, dressed in an authentic engineer's uniform, with elbow resting on the window opening, waves from the cab. More than a hundred hands return his wave from the platform. The continuous gong of the bell supercharges the enthusiasm of the crowd.

Finally, with a squeal, the brakes engage. The eight huge driver wheels grind to a halt. *Mountain Thunder*, the mighty steam engine, sits motionless, hissing, puffing and snorting, as if taking a breather after strenuous exercise.

The mighty Mountain Thunder arrives at the Queen City Station.

A uniformed conductor, complete with stopwatch, and with a railroad badge displayed on his hat, greets the passengers as we enter the coaches through the vestibule.

At precisely the appointed time, his voice echoes up and down the platform, "All 'board!"

The warning of the whistle signals our departure from the station. Within a few minutes, the train crosses Wills Creek and begins to pass through the narrows, a natural cut in the Allegheny Front between Wills and Haystack Mountains. We then begin to climb in elevation. The rails snake through a path cut into the side of the densely-wooded mountains. At times, the foliage of the sumacs, oaks and other deciduous trees brush the windows as we pass by. Bone Cave, where prehistoric remnants of times past were uncovered when the roadbed for the tracks was laid in the early 20th century, is close by to the left. The fossils of tigers and other ferocious beasts discovered in this area are now on display at the Smithsonian Museum.

The snap of the conductor's punch echoes around him as he methodically strolls down the aisle of the cars: "Tickets, please! Have your tickets ready."

At Helmstetter's Horseshoe Curve, *Mountain Thunder* is plainly visible from my window seat in the last car. A hundred or so rail buffs are gathered by a cemetery, just to the left of the tracks, to capture on photographic medium a glimpse of Number 734 as it struggles up the 2.8 percent grade. The story of *The Little Engine That Could* comes to mind. The folks behind the cameras all wave, and the riders wave back in unison.

During the minute or so trip through the nine-hundred-foot-long Brush Tunnel, the coaches are abruptly plunged into total darkness. I try to see my finger in front of my face, but it is an exercise in futility! This is as close to total darkness as one can get. A tinge of coal smoke filters into the train. No wonder, for as we exit the tunnel, I look back and see black smoke pouring from its mouth.

MONDAY - JUNE 9, 1766

"Set up the Sector in the direction of our Line at the distance of 165 miles 54 chains 88 links from the Post marked West in Mr. Bryan's field, and made the following observations..."

The train passes the village of Barrelville, about a mile-and-a-half south of the site of the June 1766 ten-day encampment of the survey party. During this time, two dozen stars were observed, and their declinations recorded. From this data, the ground position of the camp was calculated.

WEDNESDAY - JUNE 18, 1766

"Set a post (18 inches square, 3 feet in the ground and 5 above) at the distance of 3.66 chains, North of the Sector, marked M on the South Side, P on the North Side and W on the West: and began to cut a Visto in the true parallel or Line between Maryland and Pennsylvania."

The density of the forest and the ruggedness of the mountainous terrain leave me with a lasting appreciation of the difficulties the 18th century surveyors endured as they surveyed their way west. The lying of the track along this same path by 19th century railroaders, before the advent of modern earthmoving equipment, must have been an equally-arduous task. Both were truly exceptional scientific and engineering achievements of their time.

Occasionally, the air currents and the forest ceiling of leaves cause the train to become enveloped in smoke. *Mountain Thunder* chugs along—albeit at a slower pace—as it pulls the cars up yet another steep grade. To the right and below is Mount Savage. Here, in the mid-19th century, the first rails manufactured in the United States were molded from the products of local iron ore and coal mines. The piercing sound of the whistle echoes through the coaches as the train approaches sundry grade crossings.

Finally, 16 miles, 55 minutes and 1300 feet in elevation above the city of Cumberland, the train pulls into the Frostburg station, its cargo of passengers disembarking shortly thereafter. Just forward of the station by a few hundred feet is the literal end of the line. *Mountain Thunder* is uncoupled from the coaches, still hissing, snorting and gurgling as it moves forward onto the turntable. There, it is turned 180 degrees and lined up with a track parallel to its five coaches. The colossal locomotive inches forward, as both the track and the steel frame of the turntable moan and groan under the half-million pounds of iron, water and coal. About a quarter mile down the track, the locomotive is switched back onto

734 on the turntable at Frostburg.

the main line, put into reverse and re-coupled to the other end of the train.

The engineer climbs down the ladder from the cab. He is immediately cornered by a group of people. The questions come fast and furiously: "How much water does the engine carry?" "Two-thousand-five-hundred gallons," he replies. "How much coal does the *Mountain Thunder* burn on a roundtrip from Cumberland to Frostburg?" "Three tons," is his answer. "Is the bell on the engine the original?" "Don't know," he responds as he struggles to escape center stage. He successfully disappears into the crowd, only to be glimpsed later, framed in the window of the cab, enjoying an ice cream cone.

The Whistle Stop, a combination sandwich shop and craft emporium, is located immediately across Depot Street from the train station. The restaurant crew is ready, willing and able to make sandwiches and hamburgers for the crowd that descends upon them during the train's ninety-minute layover.

"All 'board for Cumberland!". Right on cue at 2 p.m., the train leaves on its return trip.

Precisely five minutes before the scheduled departure time, a high-pitched shriek of steam passing through the orifice of the whistle warns us that it is time to go. The trip back is a little easier on *Mountain Thunder*, because we are now traveling downhill on the 1300-foot difference in elevation between Frostburg and Cumberland. Three hours and thirty minutes after leaving Queen City Station, the train rolls back into town. I linger in the seat of the middle car of the train, sorry that the ride is over. Indeed, it was a trip into times past, and I plan to be back again.

The Western Maryland Scenic Railroad excursion trains run from May through mid-December. The schedule varies. A diesel locomotive is used on weekdays. The mighty steam engine named *Mountain Thunder*, rescued from the mothballs of retirement, proudly powers the train on Fridays, Saturdays and Sundays. Parking is free in the lot across the street from the Queen City Station.

FRIDAY - NOVEMBER 21, 1766

"Attended the Gentlemen Commissioners At this Meeting the Commissioners agreed we should immediately proceed to extend the West Line (from the Post Marked West in Mr. Bryan's field) Eastward to the River Delaware. And also Resolved that General Johnson (His Majesty's Agent for Indian Affairs) should be applied to (if they will not sell their Land) for to gain the consent of the Six Nations to lets us continue the West Line to the extent of the Provinces."

Penn's land grant from Charles II specified the western limit of his province to be **"... five degrees in longitude from the River Delaware."** This is yet another example of an ambiguous definition of borders. Interpreted literally, the western border of Pennsylvania would be an irregular line that mirrored the snaking curves of the Delaware, several hundred miles to the east. For many years, this wasn't much of an issue, as there were few inhabitants in the lands west of Cumberland. Virginia stepped into the void, and on numerous occasions claimed various borders that infringed upon Penn's grant. Most, but not all, of the proprietors of Virginia finally agreed that the western border would be a meridian—a north-south line—drawn at five degrees longitude from where the southern border of Pennsylvania, if extended eastward, would intersect the Delaware River. Within a few days of the November 21st meeting with the Commissioners, the survey crew took up the task of extending the parallel of latitude eastward, across the city of Wilmington, from the Post Mark'd West to the Delaware River—a distance of a little over eleven miles. The ultimate objective of this work was to eventually measure the distance of five degrees longitude from the river to the western limits of Pennsylvania, as provided for in Penn's charter of 1681.

SUNDAY - NOVEMBER 30, 1766

"Placed a mark in the Line on the Bank of the Delaware"

The call was an easy one for the now seasoned surveyors. It took them only six days to complete the task. The mark on the bank of the Delaware was placed on the north bank of Christiana Creek—by today's reckoning the Christiana River—where it emptied into the Delaware. A lighthouse, illuminating the entrance to the Port of Wilmington, now sits near this spot. It is on Cherry Island, a spoil area for the deposit of sludge dredged up from the bottom of the Delaware River channel. From the north, access is impossible, because it would be directly through the Wilmington sewerage disposal plant. Across the Christiana are the docks of the Port of Wilmington. I attempt to gain admittance through the controlled entrance of the port area in hope of snapping a photo of the lighthouse. My powers of persuasion prove no match for the resolve of the guard, who isn't about to allow anyone to enter the premises without good reason. My desire to take pictures arouses even more suspicion. Being a bit pressed for time, I leave before I cause a repeat of the events during my picture-taking at Camp David.

Early in December, with their year's work completed, Mason and Dixon retired for the winter to the comforts of the Harland Farm, near the forks of the Brandywine. Actually, "retired" is not the proper description, for there are many pages of notes in Mason's journal indicating that he observed the heavens on almost every clear evening. He also meticulously noted the high and low ambient temperatures, both outside and inside the observatory, for almost every day between December and the end of March. It was a typical eastern Pennsylvania winter, with temperatures ranging from near 0 degrees Fahrenheit on some nights to 60 degrees on some sunny afternoons. Time was also spent calculating the distance between successive degrees of latitude. The conclusion:

AN UNDATED JOURNAL ENTRY
"Length of a Degree = 68 miles 57 chains 65 links = 68.7206 miles"

The Year Of 1767

⸺ THE FINAL PUSH WEST ⸺

THURSDAY - JUNE 2, 1767

"An Express from Sir. William Johnson acquainted the Commissioners he had made an agreement with the Indians for to let us continue the West Line"

During the 1750s and early 1760s, Indians attacked and destroyed many of the white settlements in what is now northern West Virginia and southwestern Pennsylvania. As a peace offering to the Native Americans, King George III, in 1763, issued a Proclamation. Among other things, it forbade white settlement west of the Allegheny Mountains until additional treaties could be made with the Indians. Even though Mason and Dixon had no intention of establishing settlements in these lands, it was deemed prudent to first seek accommodation with the Cherokee, Iroquois and Shawnee, before proceeding any farther west with the survey. Thus, work on the line was slow to get started in 1767. Among other things, the men had to await an agreement with the Six Nations tribes to assist the party with their work. On June 2nd the agreement was concluded and necessary permissions to proceed were granted.

MONDAY - JUNE 15, 1767

"Sent 7 Men with the Telescope and the Sector to the Allegany Mountain where we left off last Summer"

THURSDAY - JUNE 18, 1767

"Attended the Gentlemen Commissioners at Chester Town . . . and received our Instructions to proceed with the West Line to the End of 5 degrees of Longitude from the River Delaware"

The men were dispatched with the survey equipment to Fort Cumberland. The two surveyors met with the commissioners of the provinces at Chestertown, Maryland on June 17th and 18th. There they received permission to extend the survey to the far corner of Pennsylvania, and they left shortly thereafter to take up the work they had called into recess exactly one year ago.

The month of June 1767 was unusually warm for this temperate area of the country. The readings of a thermometer hung in the shade of a house near Harland's Farm recorded a series of sweltering temperatures at mid-afternoon during the last days of June, which Mason duly recorded in his journal.

JUNE 1767
Mid-Afternoon Temperatures

Sunday	*6/21*	*95 F*
Monday	*6/22*	*94 F*
Tuesday	*6/23*	*96 F*
Wednesday	*6/24*	*86 F*
Thursday	*6/25*	*87 F*
Friday	*6/26*	*89 F*
Saturday	*6/27*	*91 F*
Sunday	*6/28*	*94 F*
Monday	*6/29*	*95 F*
Tuesday	*6/30*	*98.5 F*

The temperatures throughout the entire summer were recorded in the survey notes. These appeared to be the warmest continuous streak of the season, with the 30th day of June the hottest day of the summer.

⚬ BIG SAVAGE MOUNTAIN ⚬

THE EASTERN CONTINENTAL DIVIDE

SATURDAY - JUNE 14, 1766

"Went to the top of Savage Mountain, about 2 miles from the tents. From hence; to the summit of the next ridge called Little Meadow Mountain: I judge by appearance to be 5 or 6 miles: Between this (Savageor Allegany Mts.) and the said Little Meadow Mountain runs Savage River; which empties into the North Branch of the Potowmack: This is the Westernmost Waters, that runs to the Eastward in these parts. Beyond the Dividing Mountain (Savage) the waters all run to the Westward. The first of Note (which our Line would cross if continued) is the Little Yochio Geni, running into the Monaungahela, which falls into the Ohio or Allegany River at Pittsburg (about 80 miles West, and 30 or 40 North from hence) called by the French Fort Duquesne. The Ohio is Navigable for small craft by the accounts I have had from many that have

passed down it; and falls into the River Mississippi (about 36.5 degrees of North Latitude; Longitude 92 degrees from London); which empties itself into the Bay of Florida. The lands on the Monaungahela and Ohio are allowed to be the best of any in the known parts of North America; The Rivers abound with variety of Fish, and quantity almost incredible. At present the Allegany Mountains is the boundary between the Natives and strangers; in these parts of his Britanic Majesties Collonies. From the solitary tops of these mountains, the Eye gazes

The ridge where the Mason Dixon Line crosses the Eastern Continental Divide in Somerset County, Pennsylvania/Garrett County, Maryland.

round with pleasure, filling the mind with adoration to that pervading spirit that made them."

Note that this passage was written by Mason in his journal in June 1766, a year before the survey crew made their way to Savage Mountain. It was recorded on the occasion of his once again engaging in some forward exploring.

As I conducted my field research for this literary effort, my eyes were often treated to some truly magnificent scenery, encased in moments of awe and wonder. From time to time, with varying degrees of success, I have attempted to translate some of these visual delights into the written word. In the preceding excerpt, Mason painted a magnificent verbal picture of his 18th century vision from the top of Savage Mountain. In this journal entry that Mason recorded at the top of the Eastern Continental Divide, he has succeeded in describing a scene that no camera could ever adequately capture. I will not attempt to embellish his words, for in doing so I would only subtract from the beauty of this two-century-old word-picture of the sights and thoughts that he has so magnificently expressed.

TUESDAY - JULY 14, 1767
"At 168 miles, 78 chains the Top of Savage Mountain or the great dividing ridge of the Allegany Mountains"

On July 10, 1767 work on the survey of the westward line resumed

The Eastern Continental Divide on Interstate 68 at Green Lantern Road.

from the point where the group had stopped over twelve months ago. Four days later, they arrived at the top of Savage Mountain—the summit of the great dividing ridge of the Allegheny Mountains.

The ridge, where the dividing line crosses it, is accessible by hiking from the dead end of a private unimproved road that runs east off Samson Rock Road, just north of Finzel, Maryland. As the road emerges from the woods, a wide-open field comes into view. This is the final rusting place for several buses, some ancient farm equipment and a couple dozen retired lawn mowers. The summit of the mountain lies up a gentle slope, about a quarter mile in distance and about 150 feet higher up in elevation.

This is the Eastern Continental Divide. Theoretically, a rain drop falling on the eastern edge of this mountain finds its way into the Atlantic Ocean via the Chesapeake Bay; conversely, another falling on the western side of this ridge will make its way into the Monongahela River, thence to the Ohio and finally the Mississippi River, on its way to the Gulf of Mexico—referred to in Mason's journal as the Gulf of Florida. The Eastern Continental Divide, which is also the western limit of the Chesapeake Bay Watershed, is prominently identified on Interstate 68 at Green Lantern Road about three miles southwest of the Mason Dixon Line.

Rain had fallen the day before my visit. A small drainage ditch ran parallel to the interstate, just off the north shoulder of the road. I walk a couple of hundred feet from the east side, passing under the Green Lantern Road overpass. I watch as the trickle of water on the one side of the ridge flows west and on the other side as it flows east. This brings back memories of a year before, when I watched the Mississippi flow through its delta into the Gulf of Mexico, as well as childhood memories, when I fished in Chesapeake Bay. One day the rain drops that make up the trickle I am watching on the east side of the overpass will become part of the waters of the Chesapeake. Those on the other side will become the waters of the mighty Mississippi, as it flows south past St. Louis, Memphis and the city of New Orleans, ultimately emptying into the Gulf of Mexico.

⟶ GRANTSVILLE, MARYLAND ⟵

TUESDAY - JULY 28, 1767
"At 179 miles 44 chains Crossed the Little Yochio Geni"

The Yochio Geni River is today spelled quite differently—it is the Youghioghney River. The Little Yochio Geni is now known as the Casselman River. Its headwaters are

The farm on the dividing line along Route 669.

in the mountains, about ten miles southwest of Grantsville, near the town of Casselman, Maryland, and it eventually flows into the Youghioghney at the appropriately-named Confluence, Pennsylvania. The point of the survey crew's crossing of the Casselman was a few miles to the northeast of present-day Grantsville, Maryland.

In 1767, only Native Americans and a few very adventurous and courageous white settlers inhabited this wilderness. In late spring of 1755 General Edward Braddock passed through here on his way to French Fort Duquesne, which is today the site of downtown Pittsburgh. Among the 2400 soldiers in his entourage was a young aide by the name of George Washington. Thirty years later, Daniel Grant, thought to be the wealthiest man in the New World, purchased 1100 acres of land in this location, naming it Cornucopia. Grantsville is situated in the center of Grant's parcel.

THURSDAY - JULY 30, 1767
"At 182 miles 38 chains crossed a small branch running into the Little Yochio"

About a mile north of Grantsville, Route 669 quietly crosses the line. As you drive north across the dividing line there are no signs or markers advising you that you have just passed from Lord Baltimore's province into that of the Penn family. The scars of the right-of-way for the gas pipeline along with the change in color of the road paving are the only visible signs of a border. A large, picturesque red and white barn, along with several silos, stand sentinel at the spot where the eighteenth century surveyors passed through on July 30, 1767—182.6 miles from the Post Mark'd West. A few hundred yards to the west the line crosses Big Shade Run, the *"small branch running into the Little Yocho"* referred to in the journal.

⏤ THE PINNACLE OF THE DIVIDING LINE ⏤

NEGRO MOUNTAIN

SATURDAY - AUGUST 1, 1767
"At 184 miles 13 chains. The Top of Little Laurel Hill"

Laurel Hill Mountain is currently identified on maps and road guides as Negro Mountain. It is a thirty-mile-long ridge that runs on a diagonal from northeast to southwest. The highest point in Pennsylvania—Mount Davis, at 3213 feet—and the highest point in Maryland—Backbone Mountain, at 3,360 feet—are geological features located on this ridge. As one might expect, the pinnacle of the Mason Dixon Line also lies on the ridge, about a mile northeast of Hi-Point, Maryland, on Route 40 just west of Grantsville. At 2,886 feet AMSL, it is the highest point above mean sea level on the great dividing line. It passes between two small knobs on the ridge—Zehner Hill, on the Maryland side, at an elevation of 3000 feet, and Maust Hill, just inside of Pennsylvania, with an elevation of 2968 feet.

Negro Mountain is named after a brave man who had a vision that he was about to die. Nemesis was the black servant of Colonel Thomas Cresap, the frontiersman who we first encountered at Wright's Ferry on the Susquehanna River. In 1774 this was still wild and untamed country. The Native Americans were determined to evict the white European settlers who had encroached upon their lands. Cresap and a group of volunteers set out from Oldtown, Maryland on a search-and-destroy mission. Nemesis accompanied him, even though he had misgivings—something told him that he would not return. Cresap offered to leave him behind, but Nemesis insisted that he would go and fight beside his master. The group encountered the Indians on Little Laurel Hill, and in the heat of the ensuing battle Nemesis was killed. He was buried here on this ridge, and Cresap named the mountain as a memorial to his faithful servant.

A sign at the crest of the ridge on Interstate 68 reads **NEGRO MOUNTAIN - ELEVATION 3075 FEET.** A few years ago the mountain almost lost its name. In 1994 a passing motorist took note of the sign, and was offended by the name. The following year the U.S. Board on Geographic Names convened a special hearing to effect a name change to Black Hero Mountain. Private citizens, historians and officials from both Pennsylvania and Maryland appeared at the hearing, testifying in favor of retaining the name given to the mountain by Cresap two centuries prior. A Maryland archivist testified that the name Negro Mountain reflected an 18th century sensitivity to the important contribution African Americans made to early American history. The petition for the name change failed. The sign **NEGRO MOUNTAIN - ELEVATION 3075 FEET** can still be seen at the top of the ridge by 21st century I-68 travelers.

The highest point above sea level on the Mason Dixon Line is accessible, but only barely. The gateway to the pinnacle is via the unpaved trail identified as 35 Rocky Acres Road, which might very well be a private road. However, I see no signs marking it as such. The road is hazardous at the beginning, and becomes worse as I progress along its heavily-forested, mile-and-a-half length. I am certain that my car will end up impaled on the sharp point of a protruding boulder with all four of its wheels off the ground. Eventually, though, I arrive at a clearing. The GPS receiver indicates my position, and residing there, as evidence, is the Columbia Gas pipeline vista. I get out of the car to take some pictures. The only proof that anyone has previously visited this spot is the pipeline vista, the unimproved trail, Mason and Dixon's journal, and an old dilapidated barn located on the Pennsylvania side of the border.

Oops! My thoughts are racing ahead of reality. Coming south on the trail at a good clip on an all terrain vehicle is a young man. I imagine that I had perhaps tripped an alarm and been mistaken for a revenuer. Maybe he is coming to evict me, or worse yet to shoot me!

"Howdy," was his greeting. "You OK?" I told him of my mission. I had hopes of striking up a conversation, but he abruptly cut me off.

"Have a cow giving birth to a calf down the road. She needs help." With that, he disappeared just as quickly as he had come into view.

⤙ SOMERSET COUNTY, PENNSYLVANIA ⤚

Land on the northern side of the dividing line at this point is in Somerset County, Pennsylvania. Two events of 21st century that caught worldwide attention—one miraculous and one tragic—took place not far from this mountain crest. On a Wednesday in late July 2002, the evening shift of the Quecreek Coal mine was at work about 240 feet underground. They accidentally drilled into an adjoining abandoned, flooded mine, triggering fifty million gallons of water to gush into their working space. Nine miners were instantly trapped in a 4-foot-high, 18-foot-wide air pocket. Rescuers spend four days drilling a 30-inch-wide vertical tunnel down to the miners. By late Saturday broken drill bits and other uncontrollable difficulties seemed to have sealed the fate of the trapped miners.

The symbol of the Red Oak is faith. Nine evergreens represent the individual miners, but in a larger sense they represent all of us. We all must sometimes bind ourselves together as the nine miners did when the leaves have fallen like that of the oak in autumn. When we long for the shelter of the oak to protect us from the cold and the dark we must realize that the coldest winter of our lives or the darkest of nights when there seems to be no life in the oak its roots run deep, its limbs outstretched calling us to him and in his shadow we will be reborn in the spring.

But then a miracle occurred: The headlines of the morning papers the next day proclaimed the unbelievable rescue story. Against all odds, after being imprisoned for seventy-seven hours in the tiny air pocket, in waist deep, 50-degree water, one by one, all nine miners were brought to the surface through the shaft in a bright yellow rescue capsule. The miners and the capsule become instant celebrities, and for days, every newspaper, news magazine, cable news channel and network newscast recounted and retold the story of the "Miracle at Quecreek."

About ten months before, on a beautiful, cloudless Monday morning in September, United Airlines flight 93 took off from Newark, New Jersey, en route to San Francisco. About an hour into the flight, four hijackers diverted the aircraft. Several heroic passengers attempted to wrest control of the huge Boeing 757 from the terrorists. During the ensuing struggle, the airliner plowed nose down into a reclaimed strip mine at a speed of 575 miles per hour. The impact left a crater almost one hundred feet deep. All forty-five passengers aboard the flight perished. It was on this spot that the first battle in the war against terrorism was won. A group of Americans acted, and their efforts very likely saved the White House, or perhaps the Capitol Building, in Washington from the same fate that befell the World Trade Center Buildings and the Pentagon on that morning.

⚔ Nemacolin's Path - The National Road ⚔
Friday - August 7, 1767
"Continued the Line in the direction at 189 Miles 57 Chains. The top of Winding Hill. 189 Miles 69 Chains crossed General Braddock's Road leading from Fort Cumberland to Fort Pit. 190 Miles 1 Chain crossed Ditto a second time"

American heroes died here. (l) In quiet meditation. (r)

SATURDAY - AUGUST 8, 1767
"Continued the Line. Crossed the above road a third time."

On Friday, August 7th, the group reached the top of Winding Hill. General Braddock's Road, leading from Fort Cumberland to Fort Pitt, was crossed for the first time, about 750 feet to the east of this peak. The road was crossed for a second time, on the same day, at a distance of just over 190 miles from the Post Mark'd West. The crew camped in the area overnight, and the next day the survey notes indicate that they crossed the road yet a third time.

The road was originally known as Nemacolin's Path, a Native American trail that ran between the Potomac River in Cumberland and the mouth of Redstone Creek, at the Monongahela River, the site of present-day Brownsville, Pennsylvania. The trail—initially a 12-foot-wide passage through the wilderness—was first cleared in 1749 by Nemacolin, a Delaware Indian chief, and Thomas Cresap.

The air hangs heavy with history along this road. In early summer of 1755, twelve years before Mason and Dixon and their entourage made their way across the path, General Braddock and the young army Colonel George Washington set up Bear Camp along the trail, just inside Maryland, about a mile to the east of where the trail crosses. A historical marker pinpoints the spot that their 6th camp occupied on June 20th and 21st, 1755.

The trail eventually extended to the Ohio River at Wheeling. In 1806, an Act of Congress designated it as the first road to be financed with Federal funds. By the late 1840s, the road had been extended 800 miles further to Vandalia, Illinois. At one time, its claim to fame was as "the busiest transportation route in America", as many farmers used the route to ship produce out of their own area to

The top of Winding Hill, 189 Miles, 69 Chains from the Post Mark'd West
in Mr. Bryan's field (l). George Washington slept here (r).

the larger settlements. Over the years, the road has been known by several names: Braddock's Road, Cumberland Road, National Road and Route 40. However, the name most commonly used is the National Pike.

White mile marker obelisks dot the historic highway for many miles. The distance to Wheeling appears on one side of the marker, with the distance to Cumberland on the other. These are evocative of the stone markers that were originally installed when the road between Cumberland and Wheeling was completed in about 1818. Some markers also show the distance to small towns along, or adjacent to, the route.

Over the course of time and after many improvements, many of the road's zig-zags were eliminated. Today, the dividing line crosses the thoroughfare only once, in a hollow just below the Winding Ridge Summit of the Allegheny Mountains, at an elevation of 2601 feet. Route 40 now runs parallel to the line, at a distance of approximately 200 feet, for about a half-mile.

On Friday, August 7, 1767, the survey crew passed just across the street and in front of where today is located the State Line United Methodist Church. This house of worship is barely inside Maryland, on the southwest corner of Pigs Ear Road and Route 40.

One of the 1902 dividing line stone markers is planted off the south side of the road, in the front lawn of the house next door to the church. It looks unloved and unwanted. The once proud marker of the invisible dividing line bears evidence of the years of abuse it has taken due to its precarious position just ten feet off the shoulder of the eastbound lane of Route 40. It no longer stands vertical. It bears the wounds of many collisions with cars and lawn mowing tractors. To add insult to injury an empty beer can lies next to it.

State Line United Methodist Church at the corner of Pig's Eye Road and Route 40 (l).
Ninety-six miles to Wheeling (r).

The National Pike, Route 40, is today an asphalt-paved, two-lane highway that meanders its way along much of the original trail, through many little towns, villages and hamlets in western Maryland and Pennsylvania. It is the scenic route choice for those wishing to avoid Interstate 68 in order to experience small town Americana at its finest. The scent of history is to be found everywhere along the entire length of the road. A few miles to the west is Fort Necessity, General Braddock's grave and the Mount Washington Tavern, a mid-1800s restored stagecoach stop. In the days of the horse drawn coach, long journeys were made in stages. The daily limit of one stage of the journey was about seventy-five miles—hence the term stagecoach. This stop is about midway between Cumberland and Wheeling—a two day journey.

Gas up and bed down at the same stop. If the survey party were to retrace their steps today they would walk though the back yard of the Dixie Motel. The motel/gas station/optometrist's office/snack shop was built by the Reichenbecher family in the early 1950s. It sits on the south side of the road, on a slither of land between the road and the great dividing line. The gas station, snack shop and motel are still operated by one of the family members, while another opens up the optometrist office, but only on Tuesdays. In better days, the snack shop was a restaurant, but with the completion of Interstate 68 just a mile to the south, much of the traffic on the National Road has since disappeared. At the advertised rate of $19 a night, the Englishmen and at least part of their crew—there are only six units to the motel—would probably find it to be an inexpensive and pleasant respite from their day-to-day, beds-on-the-hard-ground and infrequent river bath existence.

Mason and Dixon passed by here on August 7, 1767 (l). The Dixie Motel and gas station - still in the Reichenbecher family after half a century (r).

A sign with an arrow directs you to the **MASON DIXON LINE - 75 YARDS** ----->. When you complete phase one of your journey, another sign directs you to the right, **MONUMENT 100 YARDS** ----->. To the west, along the pipeline vista, at the top of the hill, is monument 208, as identified on the Accident, Maryland - Pennsylvania 7.5 minute series USGS map. The marker is in very good condition. In the waning sunlight of a late November afternoon, the rocks that have been mounded around it appeared light blue in color. The stone was placed in 1902 during the resurvey, and today it stands in testimony of another survey crew that passed by this very spot more than two centuries ago.

In August 2008, a construction crew excavating for a new highway near Brownsville, Pennsylvania, unearthed a five-ton cube of history made up of soil, crushed limestone and concrete pavement. The layers of the cube, from the original 19th Century limestone to the 21st Century concrete and asphalt road surface, are a window revealing a portion of the history of the National Road. The 10,000 pound slab has been moved to a site in eastern Pennsylvania to be treated, in order to preserve it for future generations. Once the process is complete, it will be carefully cut into smaller pieces and placed on display in schools and museums.

⟜ THE TOWN OF ADDISON ⟜

The first town inside Pennsylvania on the National Pike is the town of Addison—formerly known as Petersburg. This area was initially settled at about the same time that Mason and Dixon hacked their way through the nearby forest.

A 21st century bargain at $19 per night (l). A window into history—a five-ton slab of dirt, stone and concrete that affords a look two centuries back into the origins of the National Road (r). [Photo courtesy of the National Road Heritage Corridor]

Present-day Route 40 has been rerouted around the town. Addison, population 212, is on a stretch of the original path. In the 1830s the Federal government turned jurisdiction of the road over to the states. In order to cover the expense of maintaining it, the state converted it into a toll road, and tollhouses were constructed at fifteen-mile intervals to collect fees from the stagecoaches, carts, animal herds and wagons that carried commerce westward from Cumberland. The village of Petersburg was the location of the first of six toll collection points in Pennsylvania, so it became known as Gate Number One. The structure was erected in 1835 at a total cost of $1,530. William Condon was the first toll collector of record; in 1841, he reported total collected revenues of $1,758.87. The toll keeper lived in the toll collection house rent-free and received an annual salary of $200 dollars. With the advent of the railroad in the 1850s, the use of the road as a ribbon of commerce fell into a downward spiral, and by 1888 the tolls were discontinued. The tollhouses are now closed. The old Addison tollhouse—restored in 1997—is the centerpiece of the town, and is listed on the National Register of Historic Places.

On the day of my visit in late April, three women .from the Great Crossings Chapter of the Daughters of the American Revolution are sprucing up the place for Old Pike Days—an annual event celebrated in May along the entire length of the former toll road. Their presence is my good fortune as I seek shelter inside the tollbooth from a passing spring thunderstorm. One of the women graciously takes me on a personal guided tour, during which I recognize that the two fireplaces and the restored furnishings exude the same 19th century charm as when Condon and other toll collectors resided here in times past.

The tollhouse at Addison, restored by the Daughters of the American Revolution.

On the outside wall, facing the pike, a list of toll rates is posted. One cannot help but notice that as the wheels on the wagons and carts became wider, the toll became less, eventually becoming free for wheels wider than eight inches. Obviously, wider wheels inflicted less damage on the roadway surface, which consisted of gravel and stones.

Pay the toll or pay the fine! Perish the thought of attempting to evade the toll collector. Apparently, there were scoundrels in the 19th century that left the main road and traveled a side road, thereby effectively bypassing the toll booths to avoid payment. They became known as "pikers", denoting a person of questionable character.

RATES OF TOLL ON THE CUMBERLAND ROAD IN PENNSYLVANIA

Every score of sheep 6¢

Every score of hogs 6¢

Every score of cattle 12¢

Every horse and rider 4¢

Every lead or drove horse, mule or ass 3¢

Every sled or sleigh drawn by one horse or pair of oxen 3¢

Every horse or oxen additional 3¢

Every dearborne, sulky, chair or chaise with one horse 6¢

Every chariot, coach, coach chair, stage, phaeton

or chaise with two horses and four wheels 12¢

Every horse in addition 3¢

Every other carriage of pleasure by whatever name it may be called, the same according to the number of wheels and horses drawing the same

Every cart or wagon whose wheels do not exceed three inches in breadth, drawn by one horse or pair of oxen 3¢

Every horse in addition 3¢

Every cart or wagon whose wheels do exceed three inches and do not exceed four inches in breadth, drawn by one horse or pair of oxen 4¢

Every horse in addition 3¢

Every cart or wagon whose wheels do exceed four inches and do not exceed six inches in breadth, drawn by one horse or pair of oxen 3¢
Every horse in addition 3¢
Every cart or wagon whose wheels do exceed six inches and do not exceed eight inches in breadth, drawn by one horse or pair of oxen 2¢
Every horse in addition 3¢
Every cart or wagon whose wheels do exceed eight inches in breadth, drawn by one horse or pair of oxen FREE
Any person refusing or neglecting to pay toll a fine of $3.00

⊷ THE YOUGHIOGHNEY RIVER ⊷

TUESDAY - AUGUST 11, 1767
"At 194 miles 25 chains 25 links - the East Bank of the big Yochio Geni At 194 miles 28 chains 00 links - the Middle of a small Island, about 200 yards wide At 194 miles 31 chains 65 links - the West Bank of the river. the water about a foot deep"

Braddock's Run Road intersects with the National Road about a quarter of a mile east of where the latter crosses the Youghiogheny River Lake. It makes its way south, in twists and turns, past summer vacation homes and trailers. For part of the way, it hugs the west bank of the Youghiogheny, far above the floor of the valley. Eventually the asphalt paving ends, and it continues on as a gravel road. Several farms dot the countryside just north of the dividing line.

I am enjoying the scenery, not paying much attention to my location when, just past the last farm field, as the road enters a forest, I come upon the Columbia Gas Company pipeline. The GPS receiver verifies my position—39 degrees 43 minutes 17.6 seconds north latitude and, as if I needed a third confirmation of my whereabouts, just to the south of the pipeline right-of-way, on the edge of the woods, stands a stone monument with **M** engraved on the south side, **P** on the north and **1902** on the west side. Just a few feet south of the marker, on the other side of the road, is the entrance to a beautiful home—a home hidden in the shadows of the forest—the home of someone who clearly prefers to live in Maryland rather than Pennsylvania!

Less than a mile to the west of this point, the surveyors reached the east bank of the Youghiogheny River. When they crossed that waterway in 1767 it was a fordable stream about 500 feet in width and about a foot deep. Today, in late winter, spring and summer, the river is a man-made recreational lake,

This 1902 monument quietly stands watch on Braddock Run Road, attesting to the survey party's passing of this place in 1767 (l). This historical marker recalls the past at the place where the National Road crosses the Youghiogheny River (r).

more than a quarter mile wide and better than thirty feet deep at the crossing point. The lake was created when the Youghiogheny Dam was constructed by the Army Corps of Engineers near the town of Confluence, Pennsylvania. When full, it stretches sixteen miles south beyond the dam to Friendsville, Maryland. From late summer through late October each year, the water level is lowered considerably to accommodate the winter and spring run-off. Although the dam was completed in 1943, the floodgates were not closed until 1948, when the bridge carrying Route 40 over the high water mark was completed. The delay was due to the shortage of steel caused by WWII. The dam is about seven miles north of the Mason Dixon Line. Its primary purpose is flood control; however, the lake and dam's secondary functions are summer time recreation and hydroelectric power generation.

The power plant at the dam is operated by the D/R Hydro Company and, when operating at full capacity, is capable of generating twelve million watts of electrical energy—enough to fulfill the needs of about 8000 homes.

⤙ THE LOST VILLAGE OF SOMERFIELD ⤚

About two miles north of the dividing line is the site of the lost village of Somerfield. Before the dam was built and the lake formed, Somerfield sat on the east bank of the Youghiogheny River. The National Road ran down into the river valley and crossed over it on a triple arch stone bridge that connected Somerfield with the village of Jockey Hollow, on the west side of the river. The structure was dedicated on July 4, 1818, with President James Monroe and several of his

The ghosts of history congregate in this area along the National Road, where it originally crossed the Youghiogheny River. Pictured is the original stone arch bridge, built in 1818 (l). It is visible when the water level has been lowered to accommodate the winter run off. When the lake is full, the stone arch bridge, as well as the lost village of Somerfield, are under forty feet of water. An interstate highway—Guard Road— where the dividing line crosses it (r).

cabinet members in attendance for the event.

Records from the Addison Historical Society tell the story of President William McKinley spending several weeks in Somerfield each summer, where he visited with family members. While vacationing, he hung his hat in the Youghiogheny Hotel, later known as the Cornish Hotel.

In the late 1930s, the Federal Government uprooted the 176 people that called the village home, purchased all of the houses in Somerfield, and summarily had them demolished. A high-level bridge was built for Route 40 to span the quarter-mile-wide lake that was about to be created. Today, when the water level is high, the stone arch bridge disappears into the river lake. Both ends of the old Route 40, as it enters into the lake, serve as boat launching ramps. In late fall, when the water level in the lake has been lowered during periods of drought, the old roadway and bridge are exposed above the water level. In addition, some of the foundations of the homes and the sidewalks of the submerged village of Somerfield are still plainly visible.

Caney Valley Road is just west of the Route 40 crossing of Youghiogheny Lake. When you turn south onto it you will never imagine that you have just entered an interstate highway! It is asphalt-paved, but barely wide enough to accommodate two vehicles. It has no shoulder, and the un-posted speed limit is considerably less than the standard sixty-five miles per hour that exists on interstates elsewhere in Pennsylvania. Within a mile, the asphalt paving disappears and gravel forms the roadbed.

You must choose carefully where you decide to share the road with passing vehicles traveling in the opposite direction, or you might find yourself in a ditch.

Eventually I arrive at an unmarked Y intersection. To the right is a dilapidated barn and farmhouse that have seen brighter days. Across the road from them are three mailboxes, still packed with junk mail from years long past. At first glance, the road bearing to the right at the Y would seem to be the better choice, but if you choose it you will never cross the dividing line of latitude that has been the focal point of our journey. The roadway that forks to the left, Guard Road, becomes even narrower. It climbs uphill and enters a heavily forested area. The notes of the resurvey crew of 1902 suggest that the road derived its name from the Guard Family, who operated a farm in this area in the late 19th century.

When you pass the dividing line there is no **WELCOME TO MARYLAND** sign or other interstate identification sign. As a matter of fact, because the surface is gravel-paved, you can't tell where maintenance jurisdiction is handed off between states. The only way you can deduce that the red barns and farmhouse just to the west are in Maryland is that they lie just south of the gas pipeline vista. The GPS receiver reads out 39 degrees 43 minutes 19 seconds, also telling me that I am 196.5 miles from the Post Mark'd West. As evidenced by the journal entry, Charles Mason and Jeremiah Dixon passed this spot on Wednesday, August 12, 1767.

WEDNESDAY – AUGUST 12, 1767
"Continued the line. At 196 Miles 31 Chains crossed a small run."

I spend a few minutes leaning against the car while taking pictures and enjoying the serenity of this off-the-beaten-track place that I would never have known to exist had I not gone searching for it. I consider my few minutes of solitude just one of those pleasant extras that come with this project of tracing the footsteps of the 18th century surveyors.

⟿ MD - WV - PA ⟾

MONDAY - AUGUST 17, 1767
"Set up the sector in the direction of our Line at the distance of 199 miles, 63 Chains, 68 Links from the Post marked West in Mr. Bryan's field and made the following observations . . ."

MEMORANDA **1767**
"At our station where the Sector was set up on the 17th of August we were
paid a visit by 13 Delawares; one of them a Nephew of Captain Black-Jacobs, who
was killed by General Armstrong at the Kittony Town in 17___. This Nephew of
Black-Jacobs was the tallest man I have ever seen."

In mid-August, in western Pennsylvania, just after the sun slips below the western horizon, the forest comes alive with the raucous sounds of millions of night creatures. The racket created by these insects in search of mates provides the ideal cover for what is already the almost inaudible sound that you might expect to emanate from the footsteps of a Native American stalking party. Surprise, surprise! Unexpectedly, a dozen-plus-one Delaware Indians wander into the camp. Their visit makes for several tense moments as the uninvited guests mingle with the Six Nations members of the survey party. The group is now in real Indian country, where intruders are frowned upon. Many white settlers in this area have met their demise when they encroached upon the lands that the Indians rightfully claimed to be their own. The penalty is immediate and final, and there is no appeal to a higher authority. Your barns and home are burned to the ground, and your scalp is taken as a trophy. Luckily, the events of this day produced no such bloodshed, but they certainly heightened the concerns about attack that were on the minds of all participants. This event did not stop progress, but it certainly unnerved the group and spurred the party on at a faster pace.

The next eight days were spent observing the stars and making calculations to determine the true position reference the line of latitude that they are marking. Unbeknownst to them at the time, the two British mathematicians and their group of laborers had stopped close to the western border of Lord Baltimore's 1632 land grant—a line drawn true north from the headwaters of the River Potowmack. The significance of this milestone was not recorded in the survey notes, as the party was unaware of the location of the point where this meridian line intersects the east-west line being marked by their efforts.

The original commission of the surveyors was to mark the Pennsylvania-Maryland border, but it was later modified to extend to the southwest corner of Pennsylvania. The province of Maryland ends here at this spot. The Calverts, however, continued to pay half of the survey expenses. This location is about two miles southwest of the present day sleepy-hollow town of Markleysburg, Pennsylvania—population 320. Today, **X** almost marks the spot where the three states converge. An overhead high voltage electrical transmission line crosses over the gas pipeline right-of-way just a hundred feet or so east of the tri-state

Marker #34 on the Deakins Line, where it meets the Mason Dixon Line, is off the beaten path. At this point Maryland, Pennsylvania and West Virginia converge.

marker. It barely misses passing over West Virginia. I cannot help but whimsically wonder if perhaps the Mountain State slaps a tax on the flow of any electrons that pass across its borders. The GPS receiver identifies the spot as being 199.5 miles from the Post Mark'd West in Mr. Bryan's field.

Access to the marker can only be made on foot, or with a four-wheel-drive vehicle. Pennsylvania Route 281 runs south from Route 40—the National Road—and becomes the principal street through Markleysburg. At the south end of town Route 281 abruptly turns right. If you venture straight at this intersection, past the **NO OUTLET** sign, you are on Brown Road. There are no identifying signs; however, the road is pinpointed on some local maps. The paved roadway soon becomes unimproved, and eventually turns into a rough trail and then just a pair of ruts through the woods. Brown Road—there is no way of knowing if it still retains its name at this point—eventually crosses the pipeline right-of-way, but it is impossible to access this vista to the west in a vehicle, due to high earthen berms used to divert rain water runoff. However, the high voltage power line crosses the trail about 300 feet into Maryland. To the west, two ruts, more than likely produced by maintenance trucks, meander through the rock outcroppings. On this warm summer morning the continuous high pitched hiss from the power line about thirty feet above me—probably produced by insulator leakage—makes for an eerie sound in an otherwise silent forest.

The remnants of an old fence—posts only—lay directly on the great dividing line. In days past it was used to keep farm animals in either Pennsylvania or Maryland! The ruts turn and run parallel to the posts for about one hundred feet. I am about to stop and get out of the vehicle to go looking for the marker when suddenly there it is, standing silently just to my right. I am almost embarrassed—the marker saw me long before I saw it! The monument snuck up on me just as the Indians might have quietly approached the survey party in a furtive manner near this same spot more than two centuries before. The four-foot-high, tri-state stone marker can't be missed. It is plainly visible about three feet north of the tire ruts that make up the trail through the dense summertime vegetation.

The pillar is not a Mason Dixon Line marker, but rather a square stone that was installed in 1910, when the exact location of the Maryland-West Virginia border was finally settled. As one might expect, the east side is engraved **MD**; the west side **WVA**; the north side **PA - 1910**. The engravings on the south side are **#34** at the top (denoting the marker number on the MD - WV boundary) and the names of three commissioners; **Samuel S. Gannett, W. McCulloh Brown and Julius K. Monroe.**

The present day boundary between Maryland and West Virginia does not follow the border set forth in the original Calvert land grant. A meridian running north from the source of the Potomac River would cross the Mason Dixon Line about a half mile to the west of this location. The Maryland-West Virginia dividing line is a broken line that runs about one degree east of north from the south bank of the north branch of the Potomac

PART 281/WV RT 26 where it crosses the border. Note the juxtaposition of the old and the new: a weathered 1883 stone marker can be seen in the background.

River to the Pennsylvania border. It follows an old boundary known as the Deakins Line, named for Colonel Francis Deakins, an 18th century surveyor who laid out tracts of land that were granted to Revolutionary War veterans. Five offsets, ranging in length from 50 feet to almost 1000 feet, accommodate 18th and 19th century land grants made by the provinces of Maryland and Virginia. The location of the boundary was disputed for over one hundred years. In 1891, the state of Maryland petitioned the United States Supreme Court to restore its right to the lands granted to Lord Baltimore in 1632. On February 21, 1910 the court issued its decision: The line would remain in the place where Deakins had established it, the location that has been accepted for more than a century. The thirty-six mile line was resurveyed and marked later that year.

Immediately adjacent to the four foot tall marker #34, on what is known as Division Ridge, at 2,300 feet above sea level, is a small granite monument, less than twelve inches tall. A brass commemorative tablet tells its 20th century story: On the plaque is engraved the Boy Scouts emblem with the words **MASON DIXON TRAIL - BICENTENNIAL - DEDICATED OCTOBER 7, 1967,** 200 years after Charles Mason and Jeremiah Dixon's historic visit to this spot.

The survey crew broke camp on the 25th of August. A party of men was dispatched to cut trees and clear the vista to the east, all the way back to Savage Mountain. The remainder of the party continued on, with Maryland still absorbing half the cost. The territory to the west of this point and south of their line was, and would be for almost another hundred years, part of the Province of Virginia.

THURSDAY - AUGUST 27, 1767

"Continued the line
At 200 miles 17 chains entered a glade or meadow
At 200 miles 21 chains crossed a run running north
At 200 miles 30 chains left the above Glade
At 201 miles 10 chains entered the same glade a second time
At 201 miles 21 chains crossed a run running north
At 201 miles 29 chains Left the Glade. This Glade is very large both to the North and to the South of the Line"

The first road that crosses the dividing line as it passes into West Virginia is Pennsylvania Route 281, which we previously abandoned in Markleysburg. When you cross the dividing line it becomes West Virginia Route 26. The run, at 200 miles, 21 chains, was but a wet spot just off the road on the day of my visit. On the eastern edge of the road stands an eight-foot-tall, three-faced stone monument, with **PENNSYLVANIA** etched vertically into one face and **WEST VIRGINIA** on another. According to an engraving at its base, it was placed there by Woodman Lodge 226—date unknown. In its literal shadow is one of the old marker stones. The monument is so weathered that the engravings on it are scarcely legible, but among the scratchings the numbers **83** are barely discernable. One would have to guess that it might be a marker installed by the resurvey party of 1883. On the western shoulder of the road is a hard-to-read, beat-up historical marker telling us—in two sentences—the story of the Mason Dixon Line.

The gas line continues to hug the Pennsylvania side of the line. Two house trailers, complete with a compliment of frolicking youngsters, take little notice of the stranger taking pictures of the markers and signs. They play within a stone's throw of the line, just inside the state of West Virginia. A few hundred feet further down the road is the final resting place for several pieces of rusting farm equipment, which appear to have reached retirement age a long time ago.

On Flat Rock Road, about a mile west, there is an old barn that could easily pass for having been there when the surveyors journey first took them past this place on August 27, 1767. The wear and tear of time and weather has taken its toll on the structure, and it seems a miracle that a heavy, wet winter snow or a summertime stroke of lightning has not yet put it out of its misery! As identified in Mason's journal, a few hundred feet to the east of the barn is Fike Run, at 201 miles, 21 chains. It trickles north as it meanders its way toward Little Sandy Creek. The glade, at the dawn of the 21st century, is dotted with the remains of old strip mines and abandoned oil wells. It's easy to get the impression that this area was long ago ravished, raped and robbed of all it had to give, and then left to wither on the vine.

Looking to the east, there is a vista cut through the forest in a straight line as far as the eye can see. It appears to be about equal in width to the one cut by the survey crew. Obviously, it is not the result of 18th century blood, sweat and handsaws, but rather the work of crews equipped with gasoline-powered chain saws, commissioned with the task of maintaining the underground gasoline right-of-way.

⤙ THE CHEAT RIVER ⤚

The Indians that accompanied, and sometimes stalked, Mason and Dixon on their 18th century endeavor are puzzled by the strange instrument used by men who spend countless hours and countless nights gazing through it at the stars. Fast forward the clock two-and-a-third centuries: If the survey crew and the Indians were to retrace their steps today they would encounter something totally alien even to the most educated men of the era. As they passed mile number 219 from the Post Mark'd West in Mr. Bryan's field, their path along the dividing line of latitude would be blocked by a puzzling array of iron boxes with protruding wires. To the informed of the 21st century, these boxes are known as transformers. They are surrounded by a barbed-wire-tipped, ten-foot-high chain link fence designed to discourage intrusion. An 18th century surveyor who never heard of electricity and its inherent wonders and dangers might rightly ask, "Who's keeping who in or out? And Why?" Leading away from the area, like the spokes of a wheel, supported on tall steel towers, are transmission lines, energized with hundreds of thousands of volts that turn the wheels of industry and illuminate the living rooms of homes in the surrounding states. This is the

*Only a few hundred feet inside West Virginia stands the Cheat River Dam and
hydroelectric generating plant. The Indian Council meeting, detailed in Mason's journal,
probably took place at, or very near, the spot where I stood to take this picture (l). The
waters of Lake Lynn gather behind the Cheat River Dam. Vacation homes and resort
venues dot the banks of the lake (r).*

power distribution station for the Cheat River Hydroelectric Power Plant, just
out of sight beyond the tree line.

Saturday - September 12, 1767

*"At 219 miles 22 chains 25 links The East Bank of the River Cheat and at 219 miles
34 chains 50 links The West Bank of the said River. . . The water at present very low
and is contained in some places where it pretty freely runs; in about 20 yards wide
and 2 feet deep. Here 2 of the Mohawks made an objection against our passing the
River but a Council being called, the Chiefs determined we should pass."*

The river and its surroundings, looking north from the point of crossing,
appear little changed from what the group described as having seen on that
Saturday morning in 1767. On occasion, a fish breaks the surface of the knee-
deep water in its effort to snatch an insect. The banks are very heavily forested,
with squirrels darting through the oak and maple trees. In the shadows cast
by the forest, a fawn stands in the cool water and drinks her fill. I slowly move
forward to take her picture, but unfortunately step on a dry stick. The sound of
it snapping spoofs the animal, and in a split second she is gone.

Looking to the south, the scenery has changed dramatically since that
long-ago Saturday morning. Stretching from the east to the west side of the
valley's steep walls, which have been carved out over the ages by the constant flow

of water, is a man-made, 125-foot-tall wall of concrete and steel. The Allegheny Power Company's Cheat River Hydroelectric Dam was completed in 1926. On this mid-summer afternoon, through one of its sluice gates and down the hundred-foot-high spillway, tumble thousands of gallons of water a minute. When rainfall is adequate and the lake is full, the water is diverted though the turbines, which are capable of generating 52 million watts of electrical energy.

No sign of the survey party's storehouse remains at the junction of the Cheat River and Monongahela Rivers—only a clump of trees.

Above the dam is Lake Lynn, named for Albert Maxfield Lynn, the president of the West Penn Electric Company during the years when the facility was constructed. To the locals it is known as Cheat Lake, a long narrow body of water about two square miles in area. In times past both sides of the river were covered with numerous strip mines, but today its banks are lined with upscale homes.

Far below the surface of the lake, a diver would find the ruins of the Old Cheat Iron Works. In 1809, Samuel Jackson, the owner of the Laurel Iron Works, of Brownsville, Pennsylvania, purchased 274 acres of land on the west bank of the Cheat River, just south of where Mason and Dixon crossed forty-two years earlier. He had intentions of expanding the business, and for better than fifty years the mill at this site flourished. The town of Cheat Neck grew up around the smoky mill, which employed 1,200 workers at its peak. As time passed, due to a multitude of factors, the business was not able to make a profit, and finally, in 1868, it ceased operations. The old village of Cheat Neck became a ghost town, when most of its inhabitants moved north into Pennsylvania.

Below the dam, the waters of the Cheat River take many twists and turns as they wind their way to join the Monongahela River, just north of Point Marion, Pennsylvania. Railroad tracks, coal tipples and strip mines—all now abandoned—dot the landscape, remnants of an age that is but a memory. For several miles, signs below the dam and along the river banks warn fishermen and others of sudden rises in water level and drastic increases in flow volume when the floodgates at the dam are about to be opened. Klaxons (loud horns) and flashing strobe lights signal any impending release of water.

Although Mason's journal does not mention it, information from other sources tell that the only known loss of life during the four year survey occurred on September 17, 1767, somewhere in this area between the Cheat and Monongahela Rivers. Two pack horsemen, William Baker and John Carpenter, were killed when a tree fell on them.

⟶ THE MONONGAHELA RIVER ⟵

SATURDAY - SEPTEMBER 19, 1767
"Set up the Sector in the Direction of our Line at the Distance of 222 miles, 24 chains, 12 links from the Post Mark'd West in Mr. Bryan's field and made the following observations: This point is the Top of a very high, steep Bank, at the foot of which is the River Manaungahela."

After ten days of stellar observations and calculations, it was determined that they were 357 feet south of the true line of latitude. They once again made the necessary correction, and then calculated the northward offset corrections for each of the mile markers to the east, back to the point of their last observation.

Had the survey taken place two centuries later, curious residents of the village of Point Marion—less than a mile to the north, with a population of 1344—probably would have gathered to watch the stargazers. On the east bank of the Monongahela River, about 350 feet below them, they would have taken notice of the abandoned Baltimore and Ohio Railroad tracks. On the west bank of the river there is the single track of the Norfolk and Southern Railroad as it crosses from Pennsylvania into West Virginia.

Just to the north and east of their 18th century campsite, on Route 119, is Evergreen Cemetery. Among the many tombstones of veterans of both World Wars is that of Benjamin Titus. The marker notes that he died on December 17, 1849 and that his life span was ninety years, four months and fourteen days. It also indicates that he served in the Revolutionary War. He was but a lad of eight when Charles Mason and Jeremiah Dixon passed by what would one day be his final resting place.

The survey journal mentions a storehouse that was constructed by the party at the forks of the Cheat and Monongahela Rivers, a point just north of Point Marion. The zenith sector was stored at this location. Today there is no evidence of any structure at this junction of the rivers to suggest that a fragment of 18th century history was shaped at this place.

TUESDAY - SEPTEMBER 29, 1767

"Twenty-six of our Men left us; they would not pass the River for fear of the Shawnees and Delaware Indians. But we prevailed upon 15 ax men to proceed with us, and with them we continued the Line Westward in a direction found as on July 10th and the 26th of August thus."

WEDNESDAY - SEPTEMBER 30, 1767

"At 222 miles 34 chains 50 links the East Bank of the River Monaunghela. 222 miles 40 chains 25 links West Bank of Ditto. The Line crosses this River

Benjamin Titus [1759-1845].

a little to the Southward of a Right Angle to the River. The Breadth of the Right Angles about 5 chains, the Running water very low, and might be contained in the space of about 5 Yards wide and six Inches deep."

Monongahela is an Algonquin Indian word meaning "high-banks-fall-down." The waterway is one of only a few rivers in the northern hemisphere that flow from south to north. It is formed by the confluence of the Tygart and West Fork Rivers in the mountains near Fairmont, West Virginia. The "Mon" as the locals call it, was the first river in the United States to have a series of dams and locks built on it to enhance commercial river navigation. The Monongahela Navigation Company was commissioned in 1837 to begin building the first of seven locks and dams from Pittsburgh toward the West Virginia state line. This navigable waterway stretches 106 miles to downtown Pittsburgh, where it joins the Allegheny River. The two team up to form the mighty Ohio River, a major tributary of the Mississippi. The trickling stream of 1767 is today, at the point of their crossing, now a river about 600 feet wide and better than 15 feet deep, thanks to its locks and dams. The water is maintained at a depth adequate to float towboats and their fully loaded clusters of barges.

Lock and Dam #8 is just a few hundred feet north of the Mason Dixon Line. It is one of nine locks and dams on the river built by the Army Corps of Engineers which allow boats and barges to travel in a series of steps down the 147-foot gradient in pool elevation from Fairmont to Pittsburgh. This lock, also

Lock and dam #8 on the Monongagela River (l). At this junction Mason and Dixon stored the zenith sector and other instruments. The 10.1 megawatt Fort Martin coal-fired power plant on the banks of the Monongahela River (r).

known as the Point Marion Lock and Dam, raises and lowers the commercial craft that transport more than 10 million tons of marketable products though this section of the river every year. The bulk of the tonnage is coal, excavated from the many deep mines in the area. The lock at this location was rebuilt in 1994, replacing the original that was completed in 1925. The dam itself was reconstructed in 1959. Water levels are raised and lowered about fifteen feet from one pool to the other.

⇾ Fort Martin ⇽

On the west bank of the Monongahela, on the West Virginia side of the dividing line, sits the village of Fort Martin, where Colonel Charles Martin built a fort in 1769. A historical marker tells the story of three settlers being killed and seven others captured by Indians near the fort in 1779. A Methodist Episcopal Church has stood at this place since 1784.

This small hamlet's 21st century claim to fame is the Fort Martin power station. The vertical plumes of white steam that pour forth from its two colossal cooling towers stretch thousands of feet into the heavens on a windless day. They can be seen against the background of a clear blue sky for better than twenty-five miles. It is but one of the seventy-two coal-fired, power-generating plants sited on the banks of the river. The waters of the river serve two purposes: barges that ply the river deliver fuel for the plant, and water from the river is used in the steam generation process that drives its mighty turbines. The plant is capable of generating 10,107 million watts of electricity, as it consumes over 7000 tons of coal per day. This energy is delivered to the power grid which supplies energy to Pennsylvania, Maryland and West Virginia. The Fort Martin plant is owned by the Allegheny Power Company, and came on-line in 1968.

⤖ ANOTHER DISPUTED BOUNDARY ⤖

Not withstanding the land grant of 1681 given by King Charles II to the Penn family that defined its western border as *". . land to extend westward five degrees in longitude computed from the said eastern bounds. . ."* the land to the west of the Monongahela River and north of the dividing line, in 1767, was the subject of another border dispute, when both Virginia and Pennsylvania claimed it.

In the early 1750s, Virginia began casting an acquisitive eye on some of the lands granted to the Penn family under their charter. This continued for the better part of three decades. Virginia made numerous attempts—using both legal and military maneuvers—to annex parts of southwestern Pennsylvania. Several borders that would have given Virginia land north of the Mason Dixon Line were proposed. One of the more brazen proposals to be introduced would have ceded all of the lands west of the Monongahela and southwest of the Ohio River to Virginia, which considered these lands to be part of its Augusta County. This included all of the present day Pennsylvania counties of Washington and Greene, along with a portion of Allegheny County. In 1773, to counter this claim, Pennsylvania included these lands in its newly formed Westmoreland County.

Both provinces had governmental and court systems in place in this territory, and primary evidence of 18th century land grants made by the province of Virginia in southwestern Pennsylvania are abundant. In some cases, the Penn family conveyed the same parcels of land to two separate owners. These situations repeatedly fanned flames of contention, when both Virginia and Pennsylvania attempted to levy taxes in the disputed territory. To add insult to injury, Virginia attempted to conscript young men from north of the line into its militia.

The chronicles of local history are rife with stories of chaos and gunplay that took place in this region, some of which rival the adventures of cowboys out west a century later. In 1771, the king of England appointed Lord John Murray, 4th Earl of Dunmore, as governor of Virginia. He was intent on pursuing the claim to these disputed lands. Captain John Connolly, of the Virginia Militia, was dispatched to satisfy Murray's ambitions, and in late spring of 1774 Connolly's

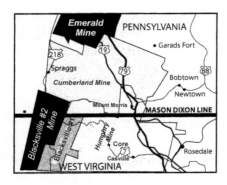

An area high in energy. The land under the Mason Dixon Line—Greene County, Pennsylvania to the north and Monongalia County, West Virginia to the south— is home to many deep coal mines that lay hundreds of feet beneath the surface. [Map by Dennis Woytek]

forces briefly took possession of Fort Pitt, at the junction of the three rivers, in what is today downtown Pittsburgh. Captain Connolly summarily renamed it Fort Dunmore. But within a few days Connolly was arrested by Pennsylvania's Westmoreland County sheriff and hauled off to prison in Hanna's Town, the county seat, located near present day Greensburg, Pennsylvania. He posted bail and was released on condition that he promise to return in September on the day set for his trial. Being an officer and a gentleman, his word was a good as gold, and he did indeed reappear on the appointed day, returning to Hanna's Town accompanied by a contingent of 150 Virginia militiamen. The court justices, along with some of the sheriff's deputies, were taken into custody and hauled off to prison in Staunton, the seat of Augusta County, Virginia.

⟿ UNDER THE LINE ⟿

WEDNESDAY - OCTOBER 7, 1767
"Continued the Line. We now have our usual compliment of Hands."

At this point in our journey we are 225 miles from the Post Mark'd West. To the south of the survey line lies Monongalia County, West Virginia— an Anglicized form of the Indian word Monongahela. To the north is Greene County, Pennsylvania, home to thick forests of deciduous trees and flowering plants, all nestled in a terrain of hills and valleys.

As the survey party hacked their way through the woodlands, up and over the hilly topography, while marking the line between Virginia and Pennsylvania, they had no recognition of the fact that 250 million years ago the ground beneath their feet was a freshwater swamp. At that time, the earth's tilt on its axis varied from what it is today, and this area was near the equator. A great variety of giant trees, mosses and ferns that would be totally alien to an 18th or even a 21st century

The now idle Humphrey Mine on the banks of the Monongahela River, just below the
Mason Dixon Line (l). Orange water (r).

woodsman thrived in the warm, humid climate. As part of their normal life cycle the trees, plants and ferns died and fell to the floor of the swampy forest, where the tropical climate caused the debris to decay rapidly and form a thick mat of peat. The stagnant water was low in oxygen content, so the decay process was due primarily to bacterial action, as opposed to the more common process of oxidation. Sediment washed over the peat. Compaction, caused by the weight of layer upon layer of peat, caused enormous pressure to build up. Physical and chemical changes took place over time, eventually causing these sediments to become transformed into coal deposits.

Today this area is a hub for coal mining and processing. West Virginia and Pennsylvania rank second and fourth, respectively, as the top coal producing states. These two counties—Monongalia and Greene—rank first as producers in their respective states and near the top in coal producing counties in the entire country. The Pittsburgh Number 8 Coal Seam, an area about ninety miles square, extends underground from just north of Pittsburgh to Clarksburg, West Virginia, and from the Appalachian Mountains into central Ohio, varying in thickness from six to ten feet. In some areas the seam is exposed at the surface. In that case, huge pieces of earthmoving equipment, called draglines, strip the overburden to expose the coal. Enormous wounds in the surface of the earth can be seen from past efforts to extract this black fossil fuel from the ground. In times past, there was little regulation of surface mining, and the exposed rubble left behind from mining efforts left a moonscape-like terrain devoid of any vegetation. Mountain streams that once flowed crystal-clear, abundant with native fish, have since been poisoned with acidic mine run off. The water, which is rusty orange in color, supports no life, and it dyes the rocks along the banks.

Lest we forget. The Robena Mine disaster that occurred 460 feet below ground level in 1962 at this very spot.

In other places, the coal seam is as far as 800 to 1000 feet below the surface. Here a gargantuan piece of longwall mining machinery continually cuts the black gold from the face of the coal seam in 100-foot swaths, leaving behind a huge underground cavern. Conveyor belts move the coal to the surface to be washed, followed by shipment to power plants and other industries. As the longwall mining machine creeps forward, roof supports are removed, allowing the ceiling in the void left behind to collapse. Woe to any structure situated above! The immediate subsidence twists, pulls and cracks foundations. Road beds crack and sink, and sinkholes occasionally gobble up cars and small buildings. Water wells go dry, utility pipes rupture, and fissures that develop from the surface down to the mine drain all of the water from streams and creeks that flow above. Today, there are laws and regulations that offer some protection to neighboring homeowners and farmers, but local news media continue to report ongoing accusations, lawsuits and disputes between surface dwellers and coal mining interests.

Several deep mines straddle the Mason Dixon Line, at depths of up to 800 feet. The historic Humphrey Mine, with its main portal in Maidsville, West Virginia, on the banks of the Monongahela River, on WV Route 100, closed permanently at the end of 2002 after all of its economically valuable coal had been extracted. The mammoth void left from the removal of millions of tons of coal during its forty-six years of operation extends ten miles into Pennsylvania. The mine produced 107 million tons of coal, which brought two-billion dollars to its owner, CONSOL Energy. Today weeds sprout up in its gated parking lot. A ten-story structure that supported the underground mining operation stands as a silent monument to an age that has since passed.

CONSOL Energy's Blacksville #2 Mine, about twenty miles to the west, is still active. Its main portal is in West Virginia, several miles beyond the end of the survey line, and it too extends far underground into Pennsylvania. Blacksville #2 opened in the 1970s, and currently operates three shifts a day, five days a week. Each shift consists of 100 workers who operate the longwall mining equipment.

More than 19,000 tons of coal is extracted each day from under the two states. While both states tax the portion of coal that is taken from under their respective lands, the mining laws of West Virginia prevail, as all of the coal exits through a portal in that state. The coal is loaded onto railroad cars and shipped via the Norfolk Southern Railway to power plants for use in the generation of electricity. The tracks were formerly owned by the Monongahela Railway, which served no less than a half dozen western Pennsylvania and northern West Virginia coal mines. A portion of the coal is exported to other countries through the Port of Baltimore. On a normal workday, it is not unusual to see a half dozen diesel locomotives struggling to pull a mile-long string of fully-loaded coal cars out of the mine.

About six miles into Pennsylvania, on northbound I-79, is the welcome center at Kirby. It is dedicated to those who lost their lives in the U.S. Steel Robena Mine on December 6, 1962, when an explosion and subsequent fire in the mine, 460 feet directly below the welcome center, took the lives of thirty-seven coal miners.

⤙ INTERSTATE 79 ⤚

THURSDAY - OCTOBER 8, 1767
"At 230 miles 22 chains. Crossed small run, running Northerly

Interstate 79 is just a little over 230 miles from the Post Mark'd West. The small run noted in the survey journal can still be seen today, trickling along on the west side of the interstate, between it and U.S. Route 19. One glance and it is evident that the highway builders used a massive amount of dynamite to blast rock for the interstate to pass this point. There is a nearly vertical seventy-five foot cliff on the eastern side of the highway where it passes from state to state. The survey crew would have had to exercise their mountain climbing skills to traverse the high, steep face of rock at this point today.

The 339-mile-long, four-lane ribbon of concrete begins near the shore of Lake Erie, in the city of Erie. It runs south through 187 miles of Pennsylvania, intersecting with I-80, I-76 and I-279 along the way before it crosses the line into West Virginia. It then continues for another 152 miles. It intersects with I-68 at Morgantown and continues to its southern terminus in the capital city of Charleston, where it ends at I-64 and I-77.

To the northwest of I-79, at Exit 1 in Pennsylvania, is the town of

Interstate 79—looking north—where it crosses the line of latitude from West Virginia into Pennsylvania.

Mount Morris. Levi Morris settled on a farm on the banks of Dunkard Creek in 1765—just two years before Mason and Dixon's visit. The town was originally named Morrisville, but its name was later changed to Mount Morris.

In the early 1800s, oil was seen oozing out of rock crevices in the area, so small holes were dug to collect what was first called "ground oil". It was primarily used as medicine. The first oil wells in this area were drilled in 1864.

Morgantown lies just to the south of the dividing line on I-79. One of the first settlers was Zaquill Morgan, who arrived in 1772. In 1785 the Virginia Assembly granted Morgan a charter for the establishment of a town to be called Morgan's Town. The area in and around Morgantown and Mount Morris was the scene of a great deal of suffering in the 1700s, as white settlers and Native Americans fought over possession of the land. Several forts were constructed in and around the vicinity as a means of protecting the settlers.

Several 19th century buildings still stand in Morgantown, the county seat of Monongalia County. Both the Old Stone House and the residence of John Rogers, prominent downtown landmarks, were built in the 1800s. The town is also the home of West Virginia University. Its medical and engineering schools are known and respected throughout the world.

⚬ BROWN'S HILL: THE END OF THE LINE ⚬

FRIDAY - OCTOBER 9, 1767

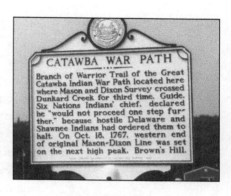

"Continued the Line to a High Ridge. At 231 miles 20 chains Crossed a War Path. At 231 miles 71 chains Dunchard Creek. This creek takes its name from a small town settled by the Dunchards near the mouth of this Creek on the Monaungahela; about 7 or 8 Miles North of where we crossed the said River. The Town was

The end of the line - "...he would not proceed with us one step farther Westward."

burnt, and most of the Inhabitants killed by the Indians in 1755. At 232 miles 43 chains crossed Dunchards Creek a second time...At 232 miles 74 chains crossed Ditto a third time. This day the Chief of the Indians which joined us on the 16th of July informed us that the above mentioned War Path was the extent of his commission from the Chiefs of the Six Nations that he should go with us, with the line; and that he would not proceed with us one step farther Westward."

The Catawba Indian War Path, at 231 miles, 20 chains from the Post Mark'd West, was the point of decision for the Indians who accompanied the group. Their concern about meeting the same fate as the Dunchards heightened their fears. An hour or so after crossing the war path they crossed the muddy, meandering Dunkard Creek for the first time, and within another mile they crossed the creek for a second time. Within 1,600 feet they came to its banks once again. Dunkard Creek is a collection of small streams that flows eastward and eventually empties into the Monongahela River, well inside Pennsylvania, crossing the dividing line no less than six times in the process.

Their amended commission had extended their surveying and marking out to the five degrees of longitude, the limit of Penn's charter. The Indians, however, had other plans, and their chief expressed them quite bluntly. The journal notes state that *"...he would not proceed with us one step farther Westward."* This literally and figuratively was the end of the line for Mason and Dixon. Their four year adventure in the New World was about to end. The survey crew set up camp on the west bank of Dunkard Creek, where it crossed the line of latitude for the

Here on Brown's Hill at 233 Miles, 17 Chains 48, Links from the Post Mark'd West in Mr. Bryan's Field, the last post on the survey line was installed on October 18, 1767.

third time.

On Saturday, October 10, 1767, the zenith sector that had been stored at the forks of the Monongahela and Cheat Rivers was retrieved, and on Sunday it was set up for the last time. During the next seven days, the stars were observed to determine the party's exact position. Subsequent calculations indicated that they were 223 feet south of the dividing line of latitude. The next day, Mason and Dixon and some of the crew proceeded seventy-four yards to the north, up the hill, to a point just east of the summit. Here at this spot, 233 miles, 17 chains, 48 links from the Post Mark'd West in Mr. Bryan's field, on October 18, 1767, the one-day-to-be-famous Charles Mason and Jeremiah Dixon planted their western-most marker—a wooden pole—with earth and stone heaped around it to a height of about five feet. This point is a few miles southwest of Mt. Morris, Pennsylvania—three miles west from where I-79 passes into West Virginia on its way south.

SUNDAY - OCTOBER 18, 1767

"The Sector stood upon a very lofty ridge, but when the Oddset was made of 3 Chains 38 Links it fell a little eastward of the Top of the Hills; we therefore extended the true Parallel 3 Chains 80 Links Westward which fell on top of the said Ridge; there, at 233 Miles 17 Chains 48 Links from the Post Mark'd West in Mr. Bryan's Field, we set up a Postmarked W on the West Side and heaped around it Earth and Stone three yards and a half diameter at the bottom and five feet High."

In the early 1800s, the Brown Family began to farm the area surrounding the end of the line. In 1883, as part of the resurvey of the Mason Dixon Line, a 30-inch-tall stone monument was placed at the site of the original wood marker post. The hill on which the engraved stone still stands was named Brown's Hill. By the mid-20th century, oil and gas wells, along with deep coal mines, dotted the area. The land eventually passed into the hands of the Consolidated Gas Company. In 1975 the 270 acres on which the Mason-Dixon Historical Park is now situated was deeded to the two adjoining counties: Monongalia County in West Virginia and Greene County in Pennsylvania. The east-west dividing line runs through the approximate center of the plot. Entrance to the park is on Buckeye Road, in the town of Core, West Virginia, just off WV Route 7. The southern portion of the park has been developed, with a baseball diamond, picnic pavilions and a century-old red barn, complete with a museum on the second floor. The northern portion of the park, in Pennsylvania, has been left undeveloped, approximating its look in the mid-18th century when the two stargazers from England traversed the lands of Maryland, Pennsylvania and, what was then, Virginia.

Connie Ammons is the manager of the park. On a cool October morning, more than two-and-one-quarter centuries after the Indians refused to "...*proceed...one step farther...*" she pilots us in a John Deere Gator, an all-wheel-drive farm vehicle. We proceed along a muddy trail that hugs the west bank of Dunkard Creek, an area of the park that supports a dense hardwood forest. The terrain immediately adjacent to the trail slopes abruptly upward, rising several hundred feet within a half-mile. We stop at a spot along the creek bank, and Connie and I poke around in the loose dirt by the side of the trail. She picks up a small fragment of an animal bone and in jest presents it to me as a souvenir of my visit. Finally I have the artifact from one of the survey party's campsites that I have been seeking for over 300 miles. Perhaps I am holding in my hand what remains of a lamb chop dinner once enjoyed by the survey crew! Then again, it may be the remains of some hapless animal that served as a meal to a natural predator. I opt to believe the former explanation.

We continue our fall jaunt, which soon takes us about 1500 feet to the west. The engine in the Gator struggles to propel us up from the bank of the creek at 940 feet above sea level to an elevation of almost 1300 feet. We pause at a spot near the summit of Brown's Hill. There, standing proudly, just as it has for more than a century, is the stone monument engraved with the numerals **1883** on its eastern face. Although weather-beaten, the letters **WV** are plainly visible on its southern face. The side of the marker that faces north has paid the highest penalty for almost 125 years of exposure to wind and rain. The letter **P** on the Pennsylvania side is barely distinguishable to the eye, but I am able to detect the engraving made in a time long past by running my fingers across the northern surface.

The original post at this spot marked the dividing line between the province of Virginia and the land granted to the Penn family. The present stone monument was installed during a resurvey of the line twenty years after the northwestern counties of Virginia separated from the commonwealth and became the 35th state of the Union.

Adjacent to the stone, 50 feet to the east and about 100 feet to the west, are two enormous Northern Red Oak trees. Their girth would suggest that they may have witnessed the historic incidents that took place within their shadow for hundreds of years. The larger of the two measures 19 feet in circumference—6 feet in diameter—about 5 feet up from the ground. A dendrologist later estimates that it is well over 400 years old. Perhaps one day, when nature claims it, and acorns no longer fall from its branches, its rings will be counted and its exact age calculated. Only then can we be certain that it was witness to Mason and Dixon's passage.

Meanwhile, here I am, on a 21st century October morning, standing at the peak of Brown's Hill. Swirling around me is a whirlwind of oak and maple leaves being propelled by a stiff breeze. My GPS receiver indicates that I am at north latitude 39 degrees 43 minutes 17.2 seconds, a little more than 100 feet south of the Post Mark'd West—the stone anchor point 233.3 miles to the east where the adventures of the two Englishmen had started three-and-one-half years earlier. This monument marks the spot where the efforts of Charles Mason and Jeremiah Dixon concluded one of the most famous of surveys ever undertaken in 18th century America.

⊷ STRETCHING THE LINE ⊷

At times during the Civil War, the Mason and Dixon Line was referred to as the dividing line between the Union and the Confederacy, or alternately as the dividing line between the Free and Slave States. Some have stretched the line east, by having it pass through New Jersey, and west as far as Missouri. The fact of the matter is, Charles Mason and Jeremiah Dixon surveyed and marked the Tangent Line, from the mid-point of the Transpeninsula Line to a point tangent to the twelve mile circular boundary of northern Delaware, identifying the western limit of Delaware from the lands of Maryland, a distance of about 82 miles; the true north-south line from the tangent to the east-west line, a distance of a little over 5 miles; a line from the Post Mark'd West east to the Delaware River, a distance of slightly more than 11.25 miles; and the great dividing east-west line of northern latitude from the Post Mark'd West to a point near Mount Morris, Pennsylvania, a distance of just over 233 miles.

As for the line serving as the dividing line between slave and free states during the Civil War, it is simply not so! The state of West Virginia, the majority of which is south of the line, was carved out of the northwestern counties of the

The less than impressive historical marker on RT 2 in West Virginia (l). Christ Church Burial Ground—Fifth and Arch Streets—Philadelphia. The final resting place of Charles Mason (r).

Province of Virginia, counties whose residents did not approve of slavery. Thus, it makes no historical sense to delineate between the free and slave states by using the Mason Dixon Line as a guide.

It was my intention when I set out to write this book to stop where the line crosses Dunkard Creek for the third time. In view of the fact that this entire effort began when I became inquisitive about the most southwestern point of Pennsylvania, I feel compelled to mention something about the last thirty-two miles. The remaining portion of the border between Virginia and Pennsylvania would have to wait almost two decades after Mason and Dixon completed their work before it would be properly surveyed and marked. David Rittenhouse and Andrew Ellicott completed the survey in 1785.

The genesis of my interest in the Mason Dixon Line was the oddity of the northern panhandle of West Virginia: Why doesn't the southwestern corner of Pennsylvania end at the Ohio River? I am driving down Route 2 along the Ohio River in the West Virginia panhandle when I come across an historical marker on the eastern side of the highway. I quickly pull off to the side of the road and make a U-turn. The words "Mason & Dixon Line" immediately catch my eye. Besides the historical marker, there is also a rather large stone monument. I could feel my adrenaline flowing! Maybe I had discovered something that I didn't already know. But as fast as the adrenaline level peaked it abruptly plummets! The stone monument marks the dividing line between Marshall and Wetzel counties, both in West Virginia. As the photo reveals, the historical marker really doesn't tell much of a story. The GPS receiver shows that I am at 39 degrees 43 minutes 14 seconds. This is very close to where the Mason Dixon Line would be if the land grant for the province of Pennsylvania had been written slightly differently to include the lands westward to the Ohio River, rather than stopping at 5 degrees in longitude from the Delaware River, and if the Indians hadn't cut the survey short at the third crossing of Dunkard Creek.

⟐ LIFE AFTER THE SURVEY ⟐

On August 27, 1768 the commissioners from the two provinces charged with overseeing the surveying and marking of the border, thoroughly pleased with the work that they had accomplished, discharged Mason and Dixon. The mathematicians/astronomers/surveyors enjoyed a few days of socializing in Philadelphia, and then traveled on to New York City. After their efforts over four years and ten months, the curtain on their adventure in America had drawn to a close. On the morning of September 11, 1768 the two set sail from New York Harbor to Falmouth, Cornwall, England aboard the Halifax packet. Mason's journal entry reads "*at 11h 30m A.M. went on Board the Halifax Packet Boat for Falmouth, Thus ends my restless progress in America.*"

The next year both men were again employed by the Royal Society to take observations of the transit of Venus across the face of the sun. Jeremiah was sent to Hammerfest, Norway, to make observations, while Charles went off to Cavan, Ireland to observe the inner planet. In the early evening of June 4, 1769, Mason observed the black disc of Venus as it passed across the surface of the brightly-illuminated setting sun. From his vantage point, some 1800 miles distant, at latitude 77 degrees north, his distinguished former partner observed the same transit planet as it passed across the disc of a sun that remained visible twenty-four hours a day during the Arctic summer. It was the last such celestial phenomena that would occur for one hundred years.

Dixon, at the tender age of thirty-seven, went into semi-retirement in 1770. He continued to sporadically practice as a surveyor in the neighborhood around his home in Cockfield. He never married, and he passed away on January 30, 1779. Jeremiah Dixon was buried in an unmarked grave in the Friends Cemetery in Staindrop, Durham, England.

Mason continued to work for the Royal Society and Royal Observatory. He remarried in 1770, and he and his new wife were the parents of five more sons and a daughter, in addition to his two sons from his first marriage. In 1786 he and his family returned to America and took up residence in Philadelphia, where he died on October 25, 1786. Charles Mason lies in an unmarked grave in the Christ Church Burial Ground, alongside other names of note such as Benjamin Franklin, John Dunlap (printer of the Declaration of Independence), Joseph Hewes and Francis Hopkinson (both signers of the Declaration of Independence), and John Ross, first husband of Betsy Ross. The cemetery is located at Fifth and Arch Streets in the City of Brotherly Love. It is just a few blocks from where the survey of the borders began—the most southern point in the City of Philadelphia in 1763—at Second and Cedar Streets.

Note: The journal of the survey, written in Mason's hand and compiled during the famous survey of the Mason Dixon Line, after twice crossing the Atlantic, remained for a time in Halifax, Nova Scotia. It came into the possession of the United States Government in 1877 and now resides in the National Archives in Washington, D.C. The journal was transcribed, under the direction of Dr. H. Hughlett Mason (not a descendent or relative of the celebrated surveyor) of the University of Virginia and printed by the American Philosophical Society in 1969. Excerpts from this publication are used herein with permission.

Appendix A

SITES ALONG THE MASON DIXON LINE

(Listed in the order in which they are mentioned in this book)

James & Ann Whitall House
Location / Directions:
Located in the Red Bank Battlefield Park,
End of Hessian Avenue at the river
100 Hessian Avenue
National Park, NJ
(856) 853-5120

Philadelphia City Hall
Location / Directions:
Broad St & Market St
Philadelphia, PA 19107
(215) 686-1776
Open Mon - Fri 8:30 a.m. - 5 p.m.

Independence Hall
Location / Directions:
6th and Market Streets Philadelphia, PA 19106
Hours of Operation: 7 days a week, opens at 8:30 a.m.
 (215) 965-7676

Liberty Bell
Location / Directions:
6th & Market Sts.
Philadelphia, PA
Open daily 9 a.m. to 5 p.m. with extended hours in July & August
The bell is visible 24 hours a day
(215) 597-8974

The Stargazer Stone
Location / Directions:
From Downingtown
South on RT 322 to PA 162 (Telegraph Road)
West (right) on PA 162 for approx 2 miles (road changes name to Embreeville Rd)
North (right) on Stargazer Rd approx 0.1 mile
The quartz stone is on the right side of the road
approx 50 ft in the front yard of a private residence.
It is protected by a two foot high stone wall.
The small plot of land that the stone is situated upon
is owned by the Chester County Historical Society.
The society also owns a right of way access from the road to the stone.

Harland Farm House
Location / Directions:
At the NE intersection of RT 162 & Stargazer Road
Private Residence
No Admittance

Post Mark'd West
Location / Directions:
Take RT 72 (Paper Mill Rd.)
North out of Newark, DE
Pass Fox Den Rd. (on the right)
Proceed approx 0.2 mile to an unpaved road on left
The road is marked White Clay Creek State Park
Proceed approx 0.2 miles to an unpaved parking area
There is a map under a glass cover that shows the location
Of the Mason-Dixon Memorial
It is a half mile (or better) walk to a pathway into
the woods - the stone is about 400 feet into the wooded area.
The park is open from dawn to dusk.

Fenwick Island Lighthouse
Location / Directions:
US RT 113 south to Shelbyville, DE
East (left) on State RT 54 for approx 10 miles to Fenwick Island, DE
South (right) on US RT 1 one block to 146th Street- west (right) on 146th Street to the lighthouse.
The grounds to the lighthouse are open to the public from dawn to dusk. The tower is closed to the public.

Historic New Castle
Location / Directions:
South on US RT 13 - pass the New Castle County Airport
At south edge of airport turn east (left) onto State RT 273 (Frenchtown Rd)
Road changes name to Delaware Street, which runs through the historic district
The old New Castle Court House, on whose spire the center of the 13-mile circular border of Delaware is drawn, is on the north side of Delaware Street.
New Castle Historical Society
2 East 4th Street, New Castle, DE
(302) 322-2794

The southwest corner of Delaware/The beginning of the Tangent Line
Location / Directions:
RT 13 south to Delmar, DE
West (right) on State RT 54
Approximately 6 miles on the north (right) side of the road
Markers are housed in a covered cage to partially protect from weather and totally protect from vandalism.

Woodland Ferry
Location / Directions:
West of Seaford, DE
Take a free ride on the Tina Fallon - a new six-vehicle cable ferry that plies the Nanticoke River from Woodland Ferry to Bethel, DE

Village of Woodland
Location / Directions:
4408 Woodland Rd.
Seaford, DE 19973
(302) 760-2080

The Woodland Ferry Association
Call (302) 629-8077 or (302) 628-0825

Henry Harrison Ross Plantation
Location/Directions:
1101 N. Pine St.
Seaford, Delaware 19973
(302) 628-9500
A restored 19th Century plantation

Chesapeake & Delaware Canal Museum
Location/Directions:
US Army Corps of Engineers
815 Bethel Rd
Chesapeake City, MD
I-95 exit 100 - State RT 279 to Elkton, MD
State RT 213 South approximately six miles to Chesapeake City
Open Monday - Friday 8 a.m. to 4 p.m.
(410) 885-5621

Chesapeake City Historical District
Guided tours are available of this restored 19th-century town.
Call (410) 885-2415 for information.

Hersch Mini Museum
Chesapeake City, MD
Features household items dating from the late 19th century and an extensive collection of irons. A partial collection of people, places, and events that have made Chesapeake City the unique place that it is today.
Tours by appointment. Call (410) 885-5889.

Conowingo Hydroelectric Dam.
Location/Directions:
US RT 30 10 miles west of Lancaster
Take I-95 to exit 85.
Follow MD 22 north to MD 136
Continue to US Route 1 north
This route will cross the Susquehanna on the Conowingo Dam.
No tours are available.

National Watch & Clock Museum
Location/Directions:
514 Poplar Street
Columbia, PA 17512
(717) 684-8261
US RT 30 ten miles west of Lancaster
Take a tour through the history of timekeeping, from early non-mechanical devices to today's atomic and radio controlled clocks.

The Wright Ferry Mansion
Location/Directions:
Columbia, PA
38 S. Second Street
Columbia, PA
(717) 684-4325
US RT 30 ten miles west of Lancaster
Restored 18th Century residence of the Wright Family
Open May through October, Tuesday, Wednesday, Friday, Saturday 10 a.m. to 3 p.m.
Admission charge

The Wedge
The ARC Corner Stone
Location/Directions:
RT 896 NW (approx 2 miles) from Newark, DE
Right on Hopkins Road, approx 0.5 miles
The stone is about 50 ft. in on the SE side of the road
The 5 foot stone marks the intersection of the two most famous borders in America—the circular northern border of Delaware and the E-W Mason-Dixon Line

Gettysburg Visitors Center
Location/Directions:
RT 30 to Gettysburg
At the center of town, turn south for approx 0.5 mile on State RT 134

Site R
Location/Directions:
State RT 16 approximately two miles east of Blue Ridge Summit
Turn south on Harbaugh Valley Rd for approximately 1.5 miles
Visitors not encouraged

Camp David
Location/Directions:
Catoctin Mountain National Park
RT 15 south from Gettysburg to Thurmont, MD
West (right) on State RT 77 (Foxville Rd) approximately two miles to park entrance on right
The park is open to the public.
The camp compound is strictly off limits to the public.

Jonathan Hager's House
Location/Directions:
110 Key Street

Hagerstown City Park

(301) 739-8393

I-81N to exit 6A Hagerstown onto US-40 E

Proceed through six stop lights, and turn right on Walnut Street.

At traffic circle, take first right exit onto Key Street (Hager House is on the right)

Hours: Tuesday-Saturday, 10 a.m. to 4 p.m. Sunday, 2 to 5 p.m.. Closed Mondays, Thanksgiving Day, Christmas Day, New Year's Day, and November 24-November 29 to prepare for Christmas.

Closed January, February and March

Fort Fredrick
Location/Directions:
11100 Fort Frederick Road

Big Pool, MD 21711

(301) 842-2155

Off I-70 twelve miles west of Hagerstown,

Take Exit 12 (Big Pool). Take State Rt. 56 south one mile

to fort entrance on right.

Visitor Center hours of operation: April 1 to Oct 31: Daily 8 a.m. to sunset; Nov. 1 to March 31: Mon-Fri: 8 a.m. to sunset; Sat-Sun 10 a.m. to sunset

Closed: Thanksgiving, Christmas Eve, and Christmas

Camping facilities available

C & O Canal Museum & Visitors Center
Location/Directions:
326 E Main St.

Hancock, MD

(301) 678-5463

Exit 3, I-70 State RT 144 west approx 0.3 miles to visitors center

Bank Road Toll House
Location/Directions:
State RT 144 at Locker Rd.
(301) 678-7377
Approx one mile west of Hancock, MD on State RT 144

Sidling Hill
Location/Directions:
3000 Sideling Hill
Hancock, MD 21750
(301) 678-5442
Six miles west of Hancock, MD where Interstate 68 cuts through Sideling Hill.
This is one of the best rock exposures in the northeastern United States. The
Exhibit Center is open daily from 9 a.m. until 5 p.m., except for major holidays.

Fort Cumberland Historical Marker
Location/Directions:
Now the site of the Emmanual Episcopal Church
Marker is located at Washington St & Cumberland St
Cumberland, MD
Original site of Fort Cumberland. The storehouse of the Ohio Company was
first located near this point in 1754

Chesapeake & Ohio Canal Museum
Location/Directions:
Queen City Railroad Station
1st Floor
13 Canal St
Cumberland, MD 21502
(301) 722-8226
I-68 exit 43C - left onto Queen City Drive
Two blocks to Baltimore Street - left to parking lot
The Visitor Center is open year round, seven days per week from 9 a.m. to 5 p.m.
Closed Thanksgiving, Christmas and New Year's Days

Western Maryland Scenic Railroad
Location/Directions
Queen City Railroad Station
13 Canal St
Cumberland, MD 21502
(301) 759-4400 or Toll-Free (800) 872-4650
I-68 exit 43C - left onto Queen City Drive
Two blocks to Baltimore Street - left to parking lot
Steam locomotive pulls the coaches Fri-Sat-Sun
The Western Maryland Scenic Railroad departs at 11:30 a.m. The round trip lasts 3 1/2 hours. Reservations are recommended, as trains can sell out. Reservations are required in October, the peak season.

The Eastern Continental Divide
Location/Directions:
Exit 29 on I-68
North on State RT 546 approx. 2 miles
Right on Sampson Rock Road approx. one mile to left 180 degree turn
Right onto unimproved road
Private property

Quecreek Mine
Location/Directions:
Follow the PA Turnpike I-70/76 to Somerset, PA
Take exit #110 - Somerset/Johnstown
Go straight out of the toll both until the first traffic light
At the light, turn left onto PA 601 North
Continue to follow PA 601 North 3.6 miles
PA 601 will then become PA 985
Follow PA 985 North for .8 miles
The memorial site is on the left, watch for the sign!
The memorial site park is open daily from dawn to dusk.
Call ahead for hours for the Visitor's and Educational Center
(814) 445 4876

Flight 93 Memorial
Location / Directions:
Flight 93 National Memorial is located in Stonycreek Township, Somerset County, Pennsylvania Turnpike exit 110 (Somerset). Straight ahead to the third traffic light, then turn onto Hwy 281 north. Drive ten miles to Stoystown. At Stoystown turn right onto US 30 east for three miles. At Highland Tank Manufacturing turn right onto Lambertsville Road. A large white states "Temporary Flight 93 Memorial" with an arrow pointing towards the road you need to take. Drive for about two miles, and then turn left onto Skyline Road. The Memorial is about a mile up the road, on the right.
The temporary memorial site at the Flight 93 National Memorial is open from dawn to dusk, 365 days per year. The site is staffed between 10:00 a.m. and 6:00 p.m. on most days during the spring, summer and fall, and between 10:00 a.m. and 4:00 p.m. during the winter months.
There are no fees to visit the Flight 93 Temporary Memorial site.
Before You Visit:
Because the Flight 93 National Memorial is located on private property, only the Temporary Memorial area is open to the public at this time. From the temporary memorial you can overlook the crash site. There is parking and several portable toilets, but no food, beverages or other services.

Nemacolin's Path - The National Road - RT 40
Location / Directions:
National Road Heritage Corridor
65 West Main Street
Second Floor
Uniontown, PA 15401
(724) 437-9877
Fax: (724) 437-6550
I-68 Exit 14A - turn left at end of ramp
I-68 Exit 14B - turn right at end of ramp
In 0.1 mile turn left onto RT 40
Note historical markers - note also restored National Road markers

Youghiogheny River Lake
The Village of Somerfield and the 1822 stone arch bridge lay under the river

Ft. Necessity National Park
1 Washington Pkwy – RT 40
Farmington, PA
(724) 329-5512
Fort Necessity National Battlefield is open daily from sunrise to sunset on a year-round basis. The Visitor Center is open from 9:00 a.m. - 5:00 p.m., except on major holidays (including George Washington's birthday).
Entrance fees to Fort Necessity National Battlefield are $5 for a seven-day admission. Children 15 and under are admitted free. Entrance is also free to anyone with a National Parks Pass.

Mt. Washington Tavern
Adjoining Fort Necessity National Park
The Mount Washington Tavern (circa 1828) catered to the stagecoach clientele in the mid-1800s and was serviced by the Good Intent Stagecoach Line.

Braddock's Grave
US Route 40 - opposite the entrance to Fort Necessity
10 miles east of Uniontown, Pennsylvania
Quietly it stands, a single marker, a reminder of a quest for empire that took place more than 200 years ago. The marker memorializes the final resting place of British Major General Edward Braddock,

Old Petersburg-Addison Toll House
Route 3002
Addison, Pennsylvania 15411 (814) 395-3550
Location / Directions:
I-68 Exit 14A - turn left at end of ramp
I-68 Exit 14B - turn right at end of ramp
In 0.1 mile turn left onto RT 40
Drive approximately ten miles to an historical marker for the tollhouse.
Bear left onto Main Street
The Old Petersburg-Addison Toll House is one of three remaining tollhouses on the National Road. Built in 1835, the tollhouse is reminder of the first interstate highway. Open for tours. Call for hours

MD-WV-PA Tri-state Marker
Marks the point on the Mason Dixon Line where the three states converge
Location / Directions:
Continue east on US Route 40 for approx 3 miles past the Youghiogheny River Lake
Turn left (south) onto PA 281
Continue to the village of Markleysburg
RT 281 makes an abrupt right turn
Stay straight on Brown Hill Road
It eventually turns into an unpaved road
Continue approx 300 feet past the MD/PA dividing line (evidenced by the gas pipeline right of way)
Turn right and drive under high voltage power lines
Follow trail approx 200 feet
Four-foot marker is on the right
Accessible by foot or four wheel drive high clearance vehicle

Cheat River Dam
Location / Directions:
Travel State RT 119 south out of Uniontown, PA approx 13 miles
Turn left on Nilan Rd (immediately before crossing the Cheat River Bridge)
Travel 3.25 miles to dam
Structure is about 100 feet inside West Virginia

Humphry Mine (abandoned)
Location / Directions:
Travel I-79 south into West Virginia
Take Exit 155 (first exit in WV)
At end of ramp turn left
Travel approx 0.2 mile to RT 7
Turn left - travel approx 0.2 miles to Rt 100
Travel approx 3 miles to Maidsville
Mine portal on the left

Robena Mine Memorial
Location / Directions:
At first rest stop inside Pennsylvania
On I-79 north

Brown's Hill
Location / Directions:
Travel I-79 south into West Virginia
Take Exit 155 (first exit in WV)
At end of ramp turn right onto RT 7
Travel RT 7 west approx 6 miles
Through the village of Core
Turn east (right) onto Buckeye Road
Travel on Buckeye approx 0.3 miles
Mason Dixon Park is on left
The last marker on Browns Hill can be accessed via a trail along Dunkard
Creek, then up 400 feet in elevation to the marker

Christ Church Burial Ground
Location / Directions:
Arch Street between 4th & 5th
Philadelphia, PA
Open March to November
Monday-Saturday - 10:00 a.m. - 4:00 p.m.
Sunday - 12:00 p.m. - 4:00 p.m.
Weather permitting
December
Sunday-Friday - 12:00 p.m. - 4:00 p.m.
Saturday - 10:00 a.m. - 4:00 p.m.
Closed January and February, Easter Sunday, Thanksgiving and Christmas.
Guided tours of the burial ground start on the hour from 10 a .m. - 3 p.m..
The historian/guide leads the visitors to markers of important Colonial and
Revolution-Era people and relates the stories of their lives. This is an excellent
way to learn about this early period of American history and become more
familiar with the lives of the American colonists.

Index

About the Author

JACK LAYTON is a broadcast engineer by trade. He owns his own business, which supplies technical consulting services to radio and television stations throughout the country. He has written several books about various broadcast related technical subjects, and has published many technical articles in nationally circulated trade journals. This is his first literary venture outside the field of broadcasting. Layton lives with his wife Cathy in suburban Pittsburgh.

The theoretical design and the empirical adjustment of a broadcast antenna system to produce certain invisible signal strength contour lines on the surface of the earth is not too far removed from the idea of using stars light years away to measure and mark invisible dividing lines on that same earthly surface. The author's inherent interest of the "whys and hows" of making the invisible visible and measurable had its genesis in a young lad of ten, and it eventually led to a career in broadcast engineering. Age has not put a damper on his inquisitiveness. The research put into the writing of this book was—in part—an effort to satisfy his never-ending curiosity of how to observe the connection between theory and reality.